The Coconut Oil Companion

Also available from Pamela Braun

High-Protein Pancakes

High-Protein Shakes

Frozen Paleo

Jerky Everything

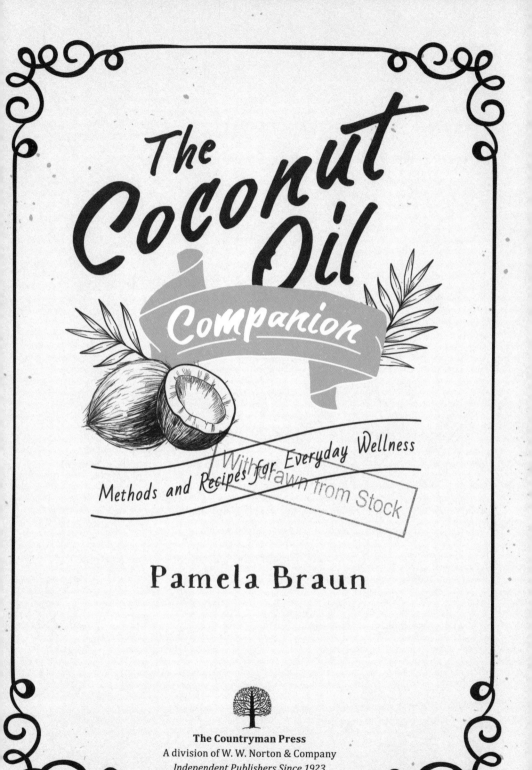

The Coconut Oil Companion

Companion

Methods and Recipes for Everyday Wellness

Pamela Braun

The Countryman Press
A division of W. W. Norton & Company
Independent Publishers Since 1923

For information about permission to reproduce selections from this book, write to
Permissions, The Countryman Press, 500 Fifth Avenue, New York, NY 10110

For information about special discounts for bulk purchases, please contact
W. W. Norton Special Sales at specialsales@wwnorton.com or 800-233-4830

Manufacturing by Versa Press
Production manager: Devon Zahn

The Countryman Press
www.countrymanpress.com

A division of W. W. Norton & Company, Inc.
500 Fifth Avenue, New York, NY 10110
www.wwnorton.com

978-1-68268-226-5 (pbk.)

10 9 8 7 6 5 4 3 2 1

CONTENTS

Part Three: Cooking and Baking

Part Four: Beauty 145

Part Five: Home 175

Part One

INTRODUCTION

Getting Started with Coconut Oil

Without a doubt, you've heard a lot about coconut oil and its various health uses lately. Although it's been used for thousands of years for a variety of purposes, only recently have we started to hear how beneficial it is. This book celebrates that, as well coconut oil's many helpful applications.

Coconut oil is the oil retrieved from matured coconuts of the coconut palm. Coconuts are actually a fruit—not a nut—and are among the most holistically useful fruits on the planet. The meat of the coconut is a high-energy, high-calorie food source. Its milk is nutritiously rich; the outer shell can be burned, turned into charcoal, or processed into other materials; the fiber is used in rope, gardening materials, and textiles; and the oil, derived from the meat, is nothing short of miraculous. Used for health and wellness, coconut oil has been shown to aid with lowering bad cholesterol and increasing good cholesterol. Studies have shown it helps with diabetes and digestion, as well as having strong antibacterial, anti-fungal, and antiviral properties. Coconut palms grow in more than ninety countries around the world, making the coconut a plentiful, stable, healthy super-fruit. This book focuses on the many amazing uses for coconut oil, from cooking and baking to household uses, health and wellness, and beauty.

Sourcing Coconut Oil

Coconut oil is readily available in most grocery stores, health food stores, and online. This section lists the different kinds one can buy (unrefined, organic virgin; refined; and fractionated), and also includes a simple DIY recipe for extracting coconut oil from a whole coconut that uses a blender and some cheesecloth.

There are three main types of coconut oil: Unrefined, Organic, Virgin Coconut Oil; Refined Coconut Oil; Fractionated Coconut Oil.

Unrefined, Organic, Virgin Coconut Oil: This is the least processed of the different types of oils. The lack of processing means that the oil retains more of its natural components and tests higher for antioxidants and nutrients. Unrefined oil is the preferred oil for use on the skin because the majority of the great properties in the oil are still intact, and it doesn't contain any other chemicals. This oil is also great for cooking. Because it is virgin oil, it will still contain some of the coconut flavor and aroma. Organic virgin coconut oil is solid at temperatures 76°F or cooler. The best organic virgin coconut oil to use is cold pressed. This type retains the most beneficial properties of the coconut oil.

Refined Coconut Oil: This oil has been processed using chemicals, heat, or other materials to refine the oil. Refined coconut oil does not contain all of the beneficial properties of virgin coconut oil because some are removed in the refining process. Refined coconut oil typically does not retain the aroma or flavor of the coconut. If using refined coconut oil, I recommend using heat- or steam-refined oil, as there are no chemicals used in this process, and therefore no chemicals would be absorbed by your body, either through your skin or by consuming the oil.

Fractionated Coconut Oil: This oil is also known as liquid coconut oil. This is coconut oil that has had its long-chain fatty acids removed via hydrolysis and steam distillation. Just by making this one change, the oil remains liquid at room temperature and extends the product's shelf life. Fractionated coconut oil is perfect for those applications in which you don't want the oil to harden. It also makes it a great carrier oil for other oils that may be used in products. While fractionated coconut oil is technically edible (if you buy food-grade fractionated oil, which is what I recommend for the recipes in this book), it is not the best for you, since the lauric acid has been removed (see the "Health and Wellness" section in this chapter for an explanation of lauric acid). You should use fractionated coconut oil in health and beauty products (where you would not want the product to harden in cooler temperatures) or for household applications.

How to Make Coconut Oil

Making your own coconut oil is a great idea, because you know what goes into it (just coconut), and the fragrance of cold-pressed coconut oil is delightful. It's also a pretty easy thing to do. The only downside to making your own coconut oil is that you only get 3 to 5 tablespoons of oil per coconut.

The first step is to get brown coconuts. Do not use young coconuts to make coconut oil. The flesh of the coconut needs to be firm to make the oil.

Crack the coconut while firmly holding the coconut in your open palm (you can also line your hand with a dish towel). Use the back side (not the blade side) of a large, heavy knife to strike the coconut and crack it. Then pour the coconut water out into a bowl and continue striking the coconut until it splits. You'll be surprised by how easy it is to break into the coconut. Set the water off to the side.

Use a dull-bladed knife to pry all the coconut meat from the shell and place it into a bowl large enough to hold all of the meat. It's okay if it has some of the brown skin on it. I try not to have too much of the skin though. You can easily cut or peel it off the meat and discard.

Chop the coconut meat into small pieces.

Place the coconut pieces and coconut water plus 1 cup of filtered water into a blender. Blitz for about 2 minutes,

until you are left with a creamy white liquid. You don't want discernible pieces of coconut in the liquid.

Pour the puréed coconut into a large bowl. Give it a good stir. The mixture should look white and creamy.

Let the bowl sit, undisturbed, for 3 hours.

After 3 hours, the coconut will separate and float to the top. For this next process, you'll need a second large bowl, a fine strainer, and two cheesecloth layers. Line the strainer with the two layers of cheesecloth and slowly pour the coconut mixture through the cheesecloth. Twist the cheesecloth to remove as much of the liquid from the coconut as you can. Discard the cheesecloth and coconut flakes.

Cover the bowl of liquid with plastic wrap and set it aside for 48 hours, then place it in the refrigerator for 3 hours, or until the top of the mixture solidifies. (These directions are presuming you are in an environment where the room temperature is around 70°F.) If you are in a much warmer environment, let the bowl sit out for 24 hours and then place in the refrigerator for 24 hours.

After it has been in the refrigerator, you'll notice a solid white mass on the top of the bowl; this is the coconut cream—the oil is just below the cream. You'll need to separate the cream from the coconut oil and water below it. Use a large spoon to scoop out the solid coconut cream

from the bowl and discard the cream. Line the strainer with another layer of cheesecloth, and carefully spoon out the oil and drop it through the strainer. This will leave you with your coconut oil.

Place the coconut oil in a lidded jar and store in the refrigerator for up to 2 weeks.

What to Look for When Buying Coconut Oil

The easiest way to make sure you are buying good-quality coconut oil is to make sure that it is non-GMO and certified organic. You also want to make sure that the oil is cold pressed and not deodorized, bleached, or made with hexane. Even when buying refined coconut oil, it should not be made with chemicals. It should be refined with heat or steam. It will say on the label if it is heat- or steam-refined.

Health and Wellness

Coconut oil is one of the richest sources of saturated fat known to man; almost 90 percent of the fatty acids in it are saturated. Although five or ten years ago, that might have scared us away from using it, new data shows that saturated fats in coconut oil have plenty of health benefits. Coconut oil doesn't contain your average saturated fats, such as the ones you would find in animal or dairy fat. Coconut oil contains medium-chain triglycerides (MCTs), which are fatty acids of a medium length. The medium-chain fatty acids in coconut oil are metabolized differently than long-chain fatty acids, such as the ones found in cheese or steak. Coconut oil contains a healthy type of saturated fatty acid (lauric acid) that your body quickly burns for energy.

As the MCTs in coconut oil break down, studies have shown that these types of healthy fats in the liver help the body burn energy more efficiently. In a 2009 study,[1] women who consumed 30 milliliters (about 2 tablespoons) of coconut oil daily for 12 weeks not only remained a steady weight, they also had lowered their abdominal fat in the process.

Coconut oil is a fat; almost 50 percent of its fat is lauric acid. The only source higher in lauric acid is breast milk. Our digestive systems convert lauric acid into a monoglyceride called monolaurin, which has antiviral and antibacterial properties. Research shows that lauric acid and monolaurin are beneficial in the fight against dangerous pathogens such as viruses, fungi, and bacteria. For example, studies have proven that these substances destroy Candida, a common source of yeast infections and the bacteria Staphylococcus Aureus.[2] Other touted benefits include uses in the early stages of cognitive diseases (the brain loves healthy fats!); increased brain function and boosted memory;[3] as a digestive aid; gum disease and tooth decay prevention; reduction in inflammation and

---

1 www.ncbi.nlm.nih.gov/pubmed/19437058

2 www.researchgate.net/publication/38019450_Glycerol_Monolaurate_and_
Dodecylglycerol_Effects_on_Staphylococcus_aureus_and_Toxic_Shock_Syndrome
_Toxin-1_In_Vitro_and_In_Vivo

3 www.tandfonline.com/doi/full/10.1080/13880209.2017.1280688

arthritis;[4] curative properties in fighting UTI's and kidney infections; a potential help in Type 2 diabetes[5] and weight loss.

Many of the recipes in this book contain essential oils (coconut oil is an excellent carrier oil for essential oils, allowing you to spread them out over your skin more evenly, see page 146). A note about essential oils: When using essential oils on your skin, make sure that you use sunscreen if you will be going outside within 24 hours of using them. Essential oils can make your skin more susceptible to burning. This includes the use of tanning beds.

I am not a licensed medical professional nor do I pretend to be one in this book. My advice, experience, and suggestions are not to be considered medical advice.

---

4 www.ncbi.nlm.nih.gov/pubmed/27878500
5 diabetes.diabetesjournals.org/content/58/11/2547.full?sid=091dd77e
-0632-4f1c-bcbd-f0b1c42544ba

Part Two

HEALTH

As we mentioned earlier, coconut oil has many health benefits. But how do you use coconut oil in ways that can improve your health? Coconut oil can play a major role in your beauty regimen.

Everything from toothpaste to makeup remover pads can be made with coconut oil—and it's so easy to do!

Toothpaste

I'll admit, using homemade coconut oil toothpaste takes a little getting used to. It doesn't taste like your typical tube toothpaste. But once you adjust to it, it's pretty great. It's a bit on the salty side, due to the baking soda, but it leaves your teeth feeling like you just left the dentist's office (minus the annoying and/or painful aspects). The ingredients in this toothpaste are all really good for you too.

I make the toothpaste without any sweeteners because I like my toothpaste unsweetened, but you could add Xylitol or a bit of liquid stevia to sweeten it up. Just go easy on the sweeteners because a little goes a long way.

Beneficial Ingredients:

- **Coconut Oil:** Naturally contains antibacterial/antimicrobial properties due to its high lauric acid content.
- **Baking Soda:** Neutralizes acid-loving bacteria in your mouth that are responsible for causing cavities. Baking soda also helps to whiten teeth, remove plaque, and maintain healthy gums.
- **Bentonite Clay:** Binds and draws out heavy metals and toxins (which is kind of a big deal when it comes to the mouth). It's alkaline and full of minerals, and it contains calcium, magnesium, and silica, all of which are good for teeth!
- **Peppermint Essential Oils:** Also have antibacterial properties.

Makes ¼ cup

1 to 2 tablespoons filtered water (amount depends on desired consistency)

2 tablespoons bentonite clay

¼ cup organic virgin coconut oil

2 tablespoons baking soda

10 to 15 drops peppermint essential oil (make sure that it is edible)

Xylitol or liquid stevia, optional (depending on the sweetness level you prefer in your toothpaste)

1. Mix the water with the bentonite clay to blend. Then mix the rest of the ingredients together until everything is mixed thoroughly.

2. You can use the toothpaste immediately after mixing. Store in an airtight container.

Note: The toothpaste will be a grayish color from the bentonite clay, so don't be concerned when it's not bright white like your regular toothpaste.

Coconut Chews

Oil pulling is the act of swishing a tablespoon of coconut oil in your mouth for 10 to 20 minutes, then spitting it out into a garbage can. (Spitting it down the sink drain can cause problems in your drain as the coconut oil builds up. Don't swallow it either.) The idea behind oil pulling is that coconut oil swished in the mouth every day helps improve oral health. Coconut oil is antimicrobial and anti-fungal, so it helps to pull the bad stuff from your teeth and gums. But you should still brush your teeth after oil pulling. I use peppermint oil in mine because it also has antimicrobial properties and helps to freshen your breath.

There aren't many scientific studies as to the benefits of oil pulling, but searching around you can find a lot of happy people who swear by the practice. Many say that they have whiter teeth, more open sinuses, reduced plaque, and less sensitive teeth. These coconut chews are an easy way to dose out a tablespoon of oil. Keeping them in the refrigerator makes grabbing one quick and easy. Just chew it up, swish it around, and you're on your way.

Makes ½ cup

½ cup organic virgin coconut oil
20 drops peppermint essential oil (make sure that it is edible)

1. Place the coconut oil in a wide-mouth glass jar along with the peppermint oil.

2. Place a jar in a saucepan filled with 1 inch of water.

3. Heat over medium heat until the oil is melted.

4. Give the oil a stir and pour into silicone molds. (I use a mold that holds exactly 1 tablespoon of liquid.)

5. Pop the molds the in refrigerator and let them harden. To speed this up, you could put the molds in the freezer.

6. Remove the chews from the molds and put in a jar. Store them in the refrigerator to keep them hardened.

Sore Throat Soother

Coconut oil is a strong anti-microbial and anti-viral that can help alleviate the pain of a sore throat. It can also help to decrease the length of a cold and help to support a strong immune system.

Makes 1 treatment

1 tablespoon organic virgin coconut oil
1 tablespoon warm water
1 teaspoon apple cider vinegar

1. Mix the coconut oil with the warm water to help melt the coconut oil.

2. Stir in the apple cider vinegar.

3. Gargle with the mixture, then spit or swallow it. Swallowing the coconut oil is beneficial for your immune system.

Athlete's Foot Massage Oil

Coconut oil has powerful antifungal properties. This is due to the presence of lauric acid. The body converts lauric acid into monolaurin, which has been shown to control the activity of bacteria, viruses, and fungi. Coconut oil has proven effective in killing the Tinea Pedis fungus (athlete's foot) and in reducing the rash caused by the fungus.

Makes 1 tablespoon

1 tablespoon organic virgin coconut oil

5 drops tea tree oil

3 drops lavender essential oil

1 drop lemon essential oil

Mix everything together and massage into dry feet.

Note: If your feet are extremely delicate, you can further dilute the essential oils down with equal parts olive oil.

Bug Repellent Balm

I was looking for a bug repellent that didn't leave me smeling like a chemical factory when I realized that I could make a nice-smelling, good-for-my-skin bug repellent that also worked. Granted, it's not as potent as those DEET-containing bug sprays, but it was far better than going with nothing—and better for me than regular bug spray.

Homemade bug repellents generally rely on essential oils for your protection. Sometimes they also use citrus oils (because they are especially potent against bugs). Be careful when using these; they can be "phototoxic," which means they can make your skin more sensitive to sunlight, and you could get a sunburn. This recipe doesn't use any citrus oils. (But if you're out in the sun, you should be using a sunscreen too.)

Since this bug repellent is creamy and absorbent, you will need to re-apply every hour if you're spending a long time outside. But it smells so good and your skin will feel so soft, you won't mind re-applying.

Makes approximately 1 cup

½ cup organic virgin coconut oil
½ cup shea butter
2 tablespoons beeswax pastilles
12 drops lemongrass essential oil
12 drops citronella essential oil
8 drops rosemary essential oil
8 drops eucalyptus essential oil
8 drops cedarwood essential oil

1. In a heatproof bowl (preferably glass) that will fit over the top of a saucepan, add the coconut oil, shea butter, and beeswax.

2. Add an inch of water to the saucepan and place the bowl on top. Heat over medium heat.

   Stir the coconut oil mixture as it melts, and continue to keep it over the heat until everything has melted.

3. Once everything has melted, remove from the heat and let rest for 3 to 5 minutes. Then stir in the essential oils.

4. Pour the balm into a jar and place in the refrigerator for at least 2 hours before using.

5. Apply all over exposed areas, and make sure to reapply if you are staying outside for a prolonged period.

Lavender Soap

Homemade soap is really popular right now. You can find it at farmers' markets and even in some grocery stores. You might even have a bar or two in your bathroom right now. But have you ever thought about making your own?

Maybe you've done the research. You've seen all the pretty bars and wanted to make it yourself, but then you read the part about lye and said, "No way." I can tell you, from personal experience, that working with lye isn't all that difficult or scary; I wanted, however, to give you a recipe that wouldn't require you to buy the lye and mix it up yourself. You can't have soap without lye, but this recipe uses bars of soap to give you a bit of a "cheat" on making your own soap.

You're adding the skin-softening coconut oil to this soap, and you can add almost any essential oil to this recipe to get the fragrance you're looking for. I used lavender because I like the way it smells, and adding the lavender buds to the top of the soap makes it look even more homemade.

Makes multiple bars of soap (depending on size of mold)

1½ cups fragrance-free soap (approximately 2 bars of soap)
¼ cup water
¼ cup organic virgin coconut oil
5 to 10 drops lavender essential oil
Food-grade lavender buds

1. Grate the soap bars on the large holes of a box grater and measure out 1½ cups.

2. Place the soap in a heat-safe bowl (preferably glass) that will fit over the top of a saucepan. Add an inch of water to the saucepan and place the bowl on top. Heat over medium heat.

3. Stir in water and add the coconut oil to the grated soap. Heat over medium heat and stir the mixture while it melts.

4. Once the mixture has melted (and it will be kind of a smooshy blob, not liquid), stir in the essential oils.

5. Spoon the melted mixture into silicone molds and sprinkle with the lavender buds. Gently pat the lavender buds into the soap so that they stick once the soap has hardened.

6. Let cool in the molds for 12 hours. Once hardened, they can be used immediately.

Alleviate Skin Irritations

Because of its anti-inflammatory properties, coconut oil has been found to help alleviate the symptoms of irritating skin conditions such as eczema and psoriasis.

Get too much sun? Coconut oil helps soothe inflamed skin, reduce redness, and rehydrate the skin.

Some breastfeeding mothers suffer from sore or cracked nipples. Applying coconut oil can help soothe and moisturize them. Plus, the coconut oil doesn't expose the baby to potentially harmful chemicals.

For skin rashes and irritations, including chicken pox and shingles, you can apply a small amount of coconut oil to the affected area to help bring relief.

Applying a small amount of coconut oil to bug bites or bee stings can help alleviate swelling and itchiness.

Prevent Ingrown Hairs

If you're not using coconut oil to shave, you may want to try it. Experience the effects of its moisturizing, lubricating, and non-irritating shave. But what can you do when you get razor bumps or ingrown hairs? That's where coconut oil comes in again. Coconut oil is healing to skin, thanks to its lauric acid content, and it has antiseptic properties which can help to heal cuts and scrapes. It also helps to keep skin moisturized.

Smooth on the coconut oil right after shaving and help to eliminate those ingrown hairs.

Deodorant

Homemade coconut oil deodorant. Now who would have thought of making their own deodorant when there are so many choices at the store? Well, for one thing, some of the ingredients in the store-bought brands aren't all that good for you. They tend to contain stuff such as aluminum (a metal that's been linked to breast cancer in women and Alzheimer's disease), phthalates (more chemicals that have been linked to fertility issues and allergy symptoms), and triclosan (which the FDA classifies as a pesticide and has been shown to have an adverse impact on thyroid hormones).

This deodorant is NOT an antiperspirant, so you will still sweat. Sweating isn't necessarily a bad thing, since it is one of the ways our body detoxes. If you find that you have sensitive skin, you can reduce the baking soda to 1 tablespoon and increase the arrowroot to 4 tablespoons.

Makes approximately ½ cup

3 tablespoons organic virgin coconut oil
2 tablespoons shea butter
3 tablespoons arrowroot powder
2 tablespoons aluminum-free baking soda
¼ teaspoon tea tree oil
Essential oils, optional (if you'd like a fragrance)

1. Place the coconut oil and the shea butter in a wide-mouth glass jar.

2. Place the jar in a saucepan filled with 1 inch of water.

3. Heat over medium heat until the oil is melted. Stir the mixture while it is melting.

4. Once it is melted, remove the jar from the pan. Stir in the arrowroot powder, baking soda, and tea tree oil (and any essential oils you may be using). Thoroughly mix this into a thick paste.

5. Scoop into a lidded jar and let cool completely before using. I like to let it cool in the refrigerator.

Reduce Blemishes

Coconut oil contains two powerhouse antimicrobials: capric acid and lauric acid. When applied to the skin, the skin converts these into monocaprin and monolaurin. These help replace the protective acid layer found on skin that gets wiped and washed away. Without the bad microbes present, acne can't form.

Coconut oil is also a great source of Vitamin E, which is essential for healthy skin. Vitamin E helps ensure that the sebum glands are working properly and aren't blocked. This helps with keeping pores open so acne can't form.

The application of coconut oil to the skin helps reduce inflammation. With the presence of coconut oil, any existing acne will become less inflamed.

Because you are using coconut oil on the skin, you should be using organic virgin coconut oil.

Coconut oil can only help in severe cases of acne. It's not a cure-all, so you should seek out a dermatologist in cases of severe acne.

Healing Detox Bath

What's more relaxing than a nice hot bath? What if you could make that bath pull double duty by relaxing you and helping you detox at the same time? This bath will do just that. Oh, and it will help to moisturize your skin, so that's a three-fer. I love taking a bath with this recipe. I feel relaxed and refreshed when I step out of the tub.

Makes approximately 1½ cups

10 drops lavender essential oil
2 tablespoons organic virgin coconut oil
1½ cups Epsom salts

1. Begin to fill the bathtub with water to your preferred temperature and add the essential oil and coconut oil to the filling tub. (This will help the coconut oil to melt quicker.)

2. Once the bath is about half-filled, add the Epsom salts to the water. Stir the water around to help the salts melt into the water.

3. Once the tub is filled, step in and let the essential oil, coconut oil, and Epsom salts work their magic. Be careful, as the coconut oil may make the tub slippery when drained.

Baby Wipes

These baby wipes have a soothing aroma and feel to them. They are not only great for the baby, but they're pretty great for anyone who's looking for a way to clean up that doesn't leave them dry and itchy.

Makes 1 roll

Paper towel roll (use "select-a-size" paper towels)
BPA-free plastic storage container (to hold wipes)
1¼ cups boiled water, cooled
2 tablespoons fractionated coconut oil
1 to 2 teaspoons baby wash
¼ teaspoon vitamin E oil

1. Using a sharp knife, cut the paper towel roll in half so that you have 2 small rolls of paper towels.

2. Place one of the half-rolls into a round 2-quart, BPA-free plastic container, cut-side down.

3. In another medium bowl, mix water, coconut oil, baby wash, and vitamin E oil. Pour mixture over the roll of paper towels.

4. Put the lid on the container and turn upside down. Let sit for 5 minutes.

5. Remove the lid from the container and carefully pull the cardboard tube out of the paper towel roll. Pull the paper towels in the center up so that they pop up like wipes. Keep the container covered when not in use.

Baby Care

Coconut oil is a great product for babies. It's all-natural and easy to use.

Cradle cap is common among babies. While it's not uncomfortable for them, the skin on their head is dry. Applying a bit of coconut oil can minimize the dry scabs on the baby's head.

Coconut oil has also been shown to be a great treatment for diaper rash because of its antibacterial and antifungal properties. It may help treat diaper rash and protect against other bacteria.

Sunburn Relief Spray

So you didn't wear sunscreen. Or maybe you did put on your sunscreen, but you stayed out well beyond the lifespan of your protection. Coconut oil is a great sunburn reliever. It helps to retain moisture in the skin, which may become dry and itchy after a sunburn. In this recipe, the coconut oil helps to rehydrate the skin while the peppermint oil soothes the inflammation. The lavender oil helps to relieve pain and disinfect the skin. While it is typically recommended to use organic virgin coconut oil, on the skin, this recipe calls for fractionated coconut oil so that the spray stays in liquid form regardless of the temperature.

Makes ½ cup

½ cup fractionated coconut oil
10 drops peppermint essential oil
10 drops lavender essential oil

Mix all ingredients together and pour into a spray bottle. Put the top onto the bottle and spray on the affected area.

Healing Lotion Bars

Homemade lotion bars are the perfect thing for keeping your hands, elbows, and feet luxuriously soft.

These lotion bars are a combination of skin-enriching ingredients. Cocoa butter (which smells amazing), coconut oil, beeswax, and almond oil. I added some lavender essential oil to mine for a more relaxing bit of moisturizing. These bars are perfect for summertime or wintertime smoothing. While the bars will stay solid in the summer heat, I prefer to keep them in the refrigerator this time of year so they're also cooling to the touch. I make mine in silicon molds, but you could also pour the liquid into lidded metal tins. This would make your lotion bars more portable.

Makes approximately 2 cups (depending on size of mold)

½ cup organic virgin coconut oil
¾ cup organic cocoa butter
½ cup beeswax pastilles
1 teaspoon essential oils, optional
1 teaspoon sweet almond oil, optional

1. In a heatproof bowl (preferably glass) that will fit over the top of a saucepan, add the coconut oil, cocoa butter, and beeswax pastilles.

2. Add an inch of water to the saucepan and place the bowl on top. Heat over medium heat.

3. Stir the coconut oil mixture as it melts and continue to keep it over the heat until everything has melted.

4. Remove from the heat and let cool for 5 minutes.

5. Stir in the essential oils and almond oil. Pour the liquid into silicon molds or lidded metal tins. Let cool until hardened.

Gum Remover

On those horrifying occasions where you find yourself with gum either stuck in your kid's hair or stuck to your carpet . . . never fear . . . coconut oil is here!

Dab a bit of coconut oil (you can use organic virgin or refined for this) onto the gum. Make sure it's fully covered, but you don't have to be extra generous with the coconut oil. Let the oil sit for 30 minutes. The oil helps to break down the gum and makes it easier to remove.

Homemade Vapor Rub

You can buy vapor rub at your local grocery or drug store, but do you really know what's in that jar? With just a few essential oils and some coconut oil, you can have a perfectly safe vapor rub, for adults anyway. It's not good to use this on children, because they can't handle the amounts of essential oils in this recipe. This recipe should also not be used by pregnant women, as the amount of essential oils is inappropriate. I like to use this when I'm working and am so stuffed-up that I can't breathe. The warmth from my chest activates the essential oils and helps to bring them up to my nose so I can breathe.

Makes 2 tablespoons

2 tablespoons organic virgin coconut oil
12 drops peppermint essential oil
12 drops lavender essential oil
12 drops pine essential oil

1. Place the coconut oil into a wide-mouth glass jar.

2. Place the jar in a saucepan filled with 1 inch of water.

3. Heat over medium heat until the oil is melted. Stir the mixture while it is melting.

4. Once it is melted, remove the jar from the pan. Let cool for about 10 minutes, then stir in the essential oils. I like to let it cool in the refrigerator.

5. Once the mixture has cooled and hardened, you can apply it to the chest.

Part Three

COOKING AND BAKING

Unlike many other cooking oils (such as olive oil), coconut oil is very stable when heated. Coconut oil can withstand high cooking temperatures, thanks to its high amount of saturated fats. It's perfect for sautéing, baking, roasting, and even frying.

Coconut oil can be used in place of other oils or fats in cooking and baking. Using unrefined organic virgin coconut oil will give your recipes a bit of a tropical flavor. If you don't like the flavor of coconut in your dishes, you can use a steam-refined coconut oil. This will give you the benefits of coconut oil without the coconut flavor. Another benefit of using the refined coconut oil is that it has a higher smoke point than unrefined coconut oil (400°F versus 350°F). This comes in handy when you're using the coconut oil to fry things.

Coconut oil can be swapped out 1:1 when using it in place of other fats in your recipes.

When it comes to butter in a recipe, I like to only swap out 50 percent of the butter for coconut oil. This helps to retain some of the buttery richness of the recipe. If you want to do a 100 percent coconut oil for butter swap, reduce the amount of coconut oil by 25 percent. This is because, unlike butter, coconut oil is almost pure fat. You may also want to add a dash of liquid to your recipe to help compensate for the moisture that butter normally adds to a recipe. There's no exact science on the liquid addition, so you'll need to play around with it.

Fudgy Brownies

There are cake-like brownies and there are fudgy brownies—the kind of brownies that are so fudgy, you wonder if they were slightly under-baked, but they weren't. These are the kinds of brownies that ooze chocolate with every satisfying bite. I didn't use all coconut oil in these brownies because I think butter brings a lot to the baked goods party, in the way of flavor. So these are made with half coconut oil and half butter. I used organic virgin coconut oil in these brownies, and you wouldn't be able to really taste the coconut in them—especially since there's a hint of espresso powder (which also helps to bring out that chocolate flavor). These brownies have a nice crunchy top and a smooth fudgy interior. This is one of my favorite recipes.

Makes 16 brownies

4 ounces unsweetened baking chocolate, finely chopped

4 tablespoons organic virgin coconut oil

4 tablespoons unsalted butter

1 teaspoon vanilla extract

1¼ cups granulated sugar

¼ teaspoon salt

2 large eggs

½ cup all-purpose flour

1 teaspoon espresso powder

⅔ cup lightly toasted walnuts or pecans, optional

1. Preheat the oven to 400°F. Line an 8-by-8-inch baking pan with foil and allow the excess to go over the sides of the pan.

2. In a microwave-safe, medium bowl, add the chocolate, coconut oil, and butter. Melt the contents of the container by microwaving, on high, in 30-second increments. Between each heating, remove the container and stir. Remove from heat when a few chunks of chocolate remain, and stir until they are melted.

3. Stir the vanilla, sugar, and salt into the chocolate. Then stir in the eggs, one at a time, then the flour, espresso powder, and nuts (if you're adding nuts). The mixture will slightly pull away from the sides of the bowl once you stir in the flour.

4. Scrape the batter into the prepared pan and bake for 20 minutes.

5. Once cool, remove the brownies from the pan, using the foil to lift them out, and cut into squares.

Pineapple Garlic Shrimp

This tropical treat will take you on a mental vacation to the islands while you eat it. Caramelizing the pineapple makes this sweet fruit even sweeter, and the garlic deepens the flavor of the shrimp. The coconut oil in this dish adds that much more to the overall tropical sensations.

You can serve this over rice or pasta. (I prefer Jasmine rice for its added flavor.)

Serves 4

¼ cup organic virgin coconut oil

¾ cup diced pineapple

10 cloves garlic, sliced

1 pound shrimp (U21–23), peeled and deveined

¼ to ½ teaspoon red chili flakes

2 teaspoons brandy

Kosher salt, to taste

Finely chopped parsley, for garnish

1. Heat the oil in a large skillet over medium heat.

2. Once the oil is hot, add the pineapple. Stir continuously until the pineapple is brown in spots. This should take about 3 to 5 minutes. Add the garlic and stir until just golden.

3. Add the shrimp and chili flakes to the skillet and toss continuously, until the shrimp are thoroughly cooked, about 2 to 3 minutes.

4. Carefully add the brandy to the skillet and stir to lift up the browned bits from the pan. Season with salt and continue to stir.

5. Serve the shrimp and sauce over rice or pasta, and top with the chopped parsley.

Coconut Granola

You might go out and buy a bag or box of granola from the store, and that's easy enough to do, but do you know what's in that granola? Lots of preservatives to help keep it nice and crunchy, even when you've left the box open for a week. Making your own granola is so easy, and it requires only the simplest ingredients. After you make your first batch, you'll become hooked on its ease and great flavor. Plus, you can make virtually any flavor combination—this recipe is merely a jumping-off point. Don't let the ingredients list put you off. You can easily find all of these items, which, most likely, will still cost less than buying that box from the store.

Makes approximately 1 quart

2 cups old-fashioned oats

¾ cup unsweetened coconut flakes

¾ cup chopped pecans

½ cup flax seeds (brown or golden)

⅓ cup sunflower seeds

1 teaspoon cinnamon

¼ teaspoon salt

4 tablespoons melted organic virgin coconut oil

½ cup grade B maple syrup

1 teaspoon vanilla extract

1. Preheat oven to 250°F. In a large bowl, stir together the oats, coconut flakes, pecans, flax seeds, sunflower seeds, cinnamon, and salt.

2. In a smaller bowl, whisk together the coconut oil, maple syrup, and vanilla.

3. Pour the coconut oil mixture over the dry mixture and stir until the dry ingredients are thoroughly coated with the wet ingredients.

4. Pour the mixture out onto a parchment-paper–lined baking sheet and spread it into an even layer.

5. Bake for 75 minutes, stirring every 15 minutes.

6. Let the granola cool completely. Break up any big clumps and store in an airtight container.

Kale with Nutritional Yeast

Kale is in the middle of its heyday right now. You'll find kale salads on just about every restaurant menu. But kale can be a hard vegetable to take sometimes, especially when it's raw. It can be tough to eat, to say nothing of the bitter taste. That's where sautéing it in a rocket-hot pan comes in. Cooked kale tends to get a bit sweeter-tasting, and while this certainly doesn't make it a dessert item, that bitter bite disappears. Once it's cooked, you can top it with all kinds of things.

For this recipe, I decided to top it with garlic and salty, cheesy nutritional yeast, which gives this vegan dish a "topped-with-cheese" flavor.

Serves 2

1 bunch lacinato (a.k.a. dinosaur) kale
1 tablespoon organic virgin coconut oil
1 clove garlic, minced
1 tablespoon nutritional yeast
Kosher salt and freshly ground black pepper, to taste

1. To clean the kale, fold the leaf over the large stalk and run your knife down the edge of the stalk. Remove the leaf and toss the stalk.

2. Once all of the stalks are removed, stack the leaves into a pile and roll them into a cylinder. Take your knife and cut the cylinder into thin strips.

3. Add the coconut oil to a large sauté pan and heat over medium heat.

4. Once the oil is hot and shimmering, add garlic. Cook for 1 minute.

5. Add the kale and cook until kale is bright green in color. You'll need to turn the kale strips several times. While it is cooking, the kale will cook down and fit into the pan better.

6. Remove from the pan and place onto a plate. Sprinkle the kale with nutritional yeast and salt and pepper to taste.

Chocolate Shell

Remember that chocolate sauce you poured over your ice cream that hardened into a magical chocolate shell? Well, now you can make that magic at home. This recipe is so easy that you'll never buy a bottle from the store again. Plus, you can make it with any type of chocolate you like. I like mine made from a dark chocolate, but you might like milk or semi-sweet chocolate. Whatever kind you like works just fine in this recipe. You can hardly call this a recipe, since there are only two ingredients. But together, they're pure magic!

Makes 2 cups

2 cups finely chopped chocolate of your choice
¼ cup organic virgin coconut oil

1. In a microwave-safe container, add the chocolate and coconut oil. Melt the contents of the container by microwaving on high in 30-second increments. Between each heating, remove the container and stir. Remove from the heat when a few chunks of chocolate remain, and stir until they are melted.

2. Let cool to room temperature or until just slightly warm to the touch.

3. Pour over ice cream. Once it turns matte, it's ready to crack into.

4. Store in a covered container on your shelf or counter. Do not store in the refrigerator. It will keep for up to 2 weeks.

Blistered Green Beans

Roasting vegetables is one of my favorite ways to cook and eat vegetables. I like how the high heat brings out the natural sweetness of the vegetables. Cooking the beans with a high heat also causes them to blister a bit and get crunchy spots, so you get a nice contrast of crunchy and soft beans. The faint coconut flavor tastes really good with the fresh beans, walnuts, parsley, and garlic.

Serves 4

1 pound fresh green beans, ends trimmed
2 tablespoons organic virgin coconut oil, melted
Kosher salt and freshly ground black pepper, to taste
1 clove garlic, minced
½ cup roughly chopped flat-leaf parsley
¾ cup toasted walnut pieces

1. Preheat the oven to 450°F. Toss the beans with the coconut oil and spread in a single layer on a large baking sheet. Sprinkle with salt and pepper.

2. Roast for 15 to 20 minutes, or until the beans are blistered in spots. You'll see some brown caramelization spots on the beans (this is a good thing).

3. Remove from the oven and sprinkle the beans with garlic and parsley.

4. Toss with the walnuts and serve warm.

Piña Colada Bread

Sure, the piña colada is a pretty tasty cocktail, but why keep that delicious combination of pineapple, coconut, and rum confined to a glass? This Piña Colada Bread is something you can eat as a snack or for a delicious breakfast. Soaking this piña colada bread in a mixture of egg and milk for a unique spin on French toast (with a little coconut syrup) could turn brunch into a decadent treat you'll want to make again and again. This piña colada bread uses a basic banana bread recipe as its starting point, but then it goes way beyond being basic. Add in macadamia nuts, coconut oil, pineapple, and coconut flakes, and you've got yourself a delicious Piña Colada Bread. The added flavor from the coconut oil is perfect.

Makes 1 (8½-by-4½-inch) loaf

BREAD

3 tablespoons organic virgin coconut oil, melted and cooled a
   bit (plus more for coating the pan)

⅔ cup granulated sugar

2 tablespoons unsalted butter, room temperature

1¾ cups all-purpose flour

1¼ teaspoons baking powder

½ teaspoon baking soda

2 large eggs

2 tablespoons full-fat coconut milk

1 tablespoon dark rum

2 really ripe bananas, peeled and mashed

½ cup crushed pineapple, drained

½ cup roughly chopped macadamia nuts

TOPPING

1 cup powdered sugar

3 tablespoons full-fat coconut milk

2 tablespoons dark rum

1½ cups unsweetened coconut flakes, toasted (see Note)

½ to ¾ cup macadamia nuts, toasted (see Note)

For Bread:

1. Preheat the oven to 350°F. Use the solid coconut oil and flour to grease and flour an 8½-by-4½-inch loaf pan.

2. In a large bowl, beat the sugar, butter, and oil on high speed for 2 to 3 minutes. The mixture should be light in color and texture.

3. Add the flour, baking powder, and baking soda to the butter mixture and blend until combined. Slowly add in the

Continued

eggs, coconut milk, and rum. Beat to thoroughly combine. Fold in the bananas, pineapple, and nuts.

4. Once everything is thoroughly combined, pour into a prepared loaf pan and spread the batter evenly in the pan.

5. Bake for 50 minutes or until a toothpick inserted in the center of the loaf comes out clean.

6. Remove from the oven and let the bread cool for 10 minutes, then remove the loaf and rest it on a cooling rack to cool completely. While the bread is baking, mix up the topping.

For Topping:

1. In a medium bowl, stir the sugar, coconut milk, and rum until everything is well combined.

2. Add the toasted coconut and macadamia nuts to the mixture and stir until everything is completely coated.

3. Once the bread has cooled, place a baking sheet underneath the cooling rack and pile the coconut and nut mixture onto the bread.

4. Let sit for at least 4 hours, so that everything firms up and it's easier to cut through the topping.

Note: To toast the coconut and macadamia nuts, heat a large skillet over medium heat. Place either the coconut or the nuts into the pan and stir until you begin to smell a toasty smell, and you see brown spots on the coconut or macadamia nuts. Remove from the pan once you observe brown spots on the majority of the mixture.

Beef with Broccoli

Tender strips of beef contrast with crisp broccoli florets, which are topped with a rich ginger and garlic sauce. All of this sits on top of a bed of fluffy rice and is the perfect beef with broccoli meal, one you can easily make at home. This simple recipe will probably find its way into your regular rotation of dinner recipes. It's easy to pull together and tastes so good.

You can use refined or organic virgin coconut oil in this recipe. The refined coconut oil works great here because there's no coconut flavor and it can withstand the higher heat of frying the meat.

Serves 4

1 pound beef (flank steak or sirloin steak)

MARINADE

2 tablespoons low-sodium soy sauce

2 teaspoons sesame oil

Freshly ground black pepper, to taste

SAUCE

1 teaspoon cornstarch

2 tablespoons low-sodium soy sauce

1 tablespoon fish sauce

2 teaspoons sesame oil

Freshly ground black pepper, to taste

Continued

BROCCOLI

2 heads broccoli, cut into florets

2 tablespoons refined coconut oil

2 cloves garlic, minced

½ teaspoon peeled and minced fresh ginger

¼ teaspoon red chili flakes

1. Slice the beef into ¼-inch-thick strips against the grain. This keeps the meat tender when it cooks.

For the Marinade:

2. Mix the marinade ingredients in a large zip top bag or

bowl and add the meat. Let the meat marinate in the refrigerator for 2 to 4 hours.

For the Sauce:

3. Mix the cornstarch with the soy sauce until it's well blended. Then add the rest of the ingredients, stir, and set aside.

For the Broccoli:

4. Place the broccoli florets in a microwave-safe bowl along with ¼ cup water and cover with a wet paper towel. Cook on high for 2 to 4 minutes (depending on how crisp you like your broccoli). The broccoli should be bright green and still crisp. Set aside.

5. Drop the coconut oil into a large sauté pan and heat over medium heat.

6. Once the oil is hot, add garlic and ginger. Stir and cook for 1 to 2 minutes, until it begins to turn golden.

7. Turn the heat to medium high and add the beef (strain off the marinade). Cook until the beef edges are crispy and turn beef over. Add the broccoli to the pan. Restir the sauce and pour it over everything in the pan. Add red pepper flakes and stir to combine.

8. Cook for 1 to 2 minutes. You should notice that the liquid thickens up a bit.

9. Remove from the heat. Serve with rice.

Orange Chicken

One of the most popular take-out dishes at a Chinese restaurant is orange chicken. You can also easily make this dish at home. Not only will you save money, but you will know what goes into it. This orange chicken dish has a tangy and slightly spicy kick to it that you and your family will really like. Use the refined coconut oil in this recipe because it will not be affected by the higher heat required to fry the chicken.

Serves 4

1 cup orange marmalade
1 teaspoon white vinegar
1 teaspoon Sriracha sauce
½ teaspoon soy sauce
⅛ teaspoon ginger powder
2 heads broccoli, cut into florets
1½ pounds chicken tenders
¾ cup refined coconut oil
½ cup cornstarch
¼ cup all-purpose flour
1 teaspoon kosher salt
¼ teaspoon freshly ground black pepper
1 large egg, beaten

1. In a medium bowl, mix the marmalade, vinegar, Sriracha sauce, soy sauce, and ginger powder. Set aside.

2. Place the broccoli florets in microwave-safe bowl along with ¼ cup water and cover with a wet paper towel. Cook

on high heat for 2 to 4 minutes (depending on how crisp you like your broccoli). The broccoli should be bright green and still crisp. Set aside.

3. Cut the chicken tenders into equal-size pieces and set aside.

4. In another medium bowl, mix the cornstarch, flour, salt, and pepper. Mix until everything is thoroughly combined.

5. Heat the oil in a deep-sided pan until it's hot and shimmery.

6. Dip 5 or 6 chicken pieces into the beaten egg and then into the cornstarch mixture. Knock off the extra cornstarch and carefully place in the hot oil. Cook for 2 to 3 minutes per side.

7. Remove the chicken from the oil and place on a paper-towel–lined plate. Continue until all of the chicken is cooked.

8. Pour the marmalade mixture into a medium saucepan. Heat over medium heat and stir until it is melted. Add broccoli and chicken to the orange mixture and stir to thoroughly coat everything.

9. Serve with or without rice.

Chocolate Chip Cookies

Some days you just want chocolate chip cookies and nothing else will do. These chocolate chip cookies will more than fulfill any cravings you have. They're rich and chocolatey, a soft cookie that has just the right amount of crunch. This is a modified version of the Betty Crocker cookie recipe. It's a great recipe because it's simple and straightforward. You can really taste the coconut in these cookies... which is a good thing, especially if you use dark chocolate chips. It adds the right amount of flavor to the cookie. If you really don't want the coconut flavor, you can use refined coconut oil in this recipe.

Makes 20 cookies

¾ cup granulated sugar
¾ cup packed dark brown sugar
¾ cup organic virgin coconut oil
1 large egg
1 teaspoon vanilla extract
2¼ cups all-purpose flour
1 teaspoon baking soda
½ teaspoon salt
1 (12-ounce) package chocolate chips

1. Mix the sugar, brown sugar, coconut oil, egg, and vanilla together in a large bowl (I used my stand mixer and paddle attachment for this recipe) and mix for 2 minutes. The sugars should take on a lighter color and slightly lighter consistency.

Continued

2. Add in the flour, baking soda, and salt. Mix for about 1 minute until everything is combined. Mix in the chocolate chips (if using a stand mixer, fold chocolate chips into the dough by hand). The dough will look crumbly—not like your usual smooth dough.

3. Form the cookies with a #2 ice cream scoop (this is your usual size ice cream scoop). Make sure the dough is pushed into the scoop well, then pop out the dough and place it onto a parchment-paper–lined plate. (The parchment paper is necessary to keep the dough from sticking to the plate. If you don't use the parchment paper, you'll need to pop the dough off the plate with a knife, which is not recommended—you could hurt your fingers.) Once the dough is on the plate, gently flatten it out a bit. These cookies don't spread much when you bake them, so you want them to have flat tops when they go into the oven.

4. Place the plate(s) in the refrigerator for 3 hours to chill.

5. Preheat oven to 375°F. Remove the plate from the refrigerator and place the cookie dough rounds onto a silicone baking sheet or parchment-paper–lined baking sheet. (I baked these 8 at a time.)

6. Bake for 8 to 11 minutes. The cookies should be light golden brown on top.

7. Remove from the oven and let cool.

Increase the Shelf Life of Eggs

How long can you keep eggs? This is a question that's almost as old as which came first . . . The first thing you should look for, when buying eggs, is the pack date. It will appear as a three-digit number. For example, if the eggs were packed on January 1, the number would be 001. The second number you might look for is the sell-by date. Not every state requires this, so you may not see this date on your eggs. This date cannot be longer than 45 days past the pack date.

The last date to look for is the expiration date. This is not federally required to be printed on the egg containers, but sometimes this date will appear instead of a sell-by date.

The standard rule of thumb for keeping eggs is to keep them 5 weeks from when you buy them. But, if you use coconut oil, you can extend the life of your eggs a little bit. All you need to do is take a bit of your coconut oil and rub it all over the eggshell and place the egg back into the carton. Oh yeah, you should not keep your eggs in the door of your refrigerator. This is the warmest place in your fridge. I know some refrigerators come with egg holders in the door, but don't use them. Keep your eggs in their carton in the main refrigerator.

Garlic Parmesan Popcorn Topping

Now that you've got your popcorn popped, what are you going to top it off with? Sure, you could use butter, but why not use coconut oil? This Garlic Parmesan Popcorn Topping is a blast of flavor. From the very first bite, you won't be able to stop eating that bowl of popcorn.

And just think, while you're snacking, you're also getting to enjoy all the health benefits of eating coconut oil.

Serves 2

¼ cup finely grated Parmesan cheese

½ teaspoon garlic powder

½ teaspoon onion powder

½ teaspoon salt

¼ cup organic virgin coconut oil, melted (or use refined oil if you prefer not to have a coconut flavor)

1. Mix the dry ingredients in a small bowl and set aside.

2. Pour half of the coconut oil over the popped popcorn and carefully mix.

3. Pour the remaining coconut oil over the popcorn and toss to coat.

4. Sprinkle the dry ingredients over the coated popcorn and gently toss to coat all of the kernels.

Coffee Creamer

By now, you've probably read about Bulletproof coffee or maybe you've even tried it. Well, you can make a similar cup of coffee using coconut oil. This recipe not only includes the coconut oil for a boost of energy, but a bit of sweetness and spice for your morning cup of java.

Makes approximately ½ cup

½ cup organic virgin coconut oil, softened
⅓ cup honey
½ teaspoon vanilla extract
¼ teaspoon cinnamon
1 cup black coffee, hot

1. Mix all of the ingredients together and make sure there are no clumps. Since it's been softened, you should be able to use a small spatula to smooth out any clumps that may show themselves in the mixture.

2. Scoop the mixture into a lidded container and seal tightly.

3. Pour the coffee into your blender and add 1 tablespoon of the creamer mixture. Buzz until everything is liquefied and smooth. (Make sure that you vent your blender when you turn it on so that the heat doesn't cause everything to explode.)

4. Pour into a cup and enjoy.

Kettle Corn

I love going to carnivals and local fairs. Why? For the kettle corn. I get the big bag and munch until my heart's content (which is usually after downing most of the bag). I can't stop eating the stuff. That salty-sweet combination is magical. This recipe lets you bring the magic of kettle corn to your kitchen. It's really quite easy to make and tastes just as good as the stuff you get at the carnival.

Serves 2

¼ cup organic virgin coconut oil
½ cup popcorn kernels
⅛ cup granulated sugar
¾ teaspoon fine-grained sea salt

1. Add the coconut oil to a 5-quart pot along with 3 popcorn kernels. Cover and heat over medium heat.

2. Once the 3 kernels pop, lift the lid and add the rest of the popcorn and evenly spread the sugar around the bottom of the pan. Cover the pan and let the popcorn start to pop.

3. While the popcorn is popping, carefully shake the pot. This helps distribute the sugar and kernels evenly in the pan.

4. Pull the pan off the heat when the popping begins to slow down. Don't wait for the popping to stop, or you'll have burnt kettle corn.

5. Quickly pour into a large bowl and sprinkle with the salt.

Mayonnaise

Yes, you can make your own mayonnaise. Why should you want to? Have you ever read the labels on those jars of mayo at the grocery store? Most of them have ingredients in them that you can't even pronounce. Making your own mayonnaise isn't hard. It takes just a few ingredients and a little bit of patience. If you're uncomfortable with the raw egg part of making your own mayonnaise, they sell pasteurized eggs that you can use so that you feel better about using them raw. It's definitely worth your time and effort to make your own mayonnaise. You can really taste the difference.

Makes 1 cup

2 large egg yolks
2 tablespoons apple cider vinegar
1 teaspoon mustard powder (I use Coleman's mustard powder)
½ cup refined coconut oil, melted but not hot
½ cup extra virgin olive oil
Salt and freshly ground black pepper, to taste

1. In the bowl of a food processor, add the egg yolks, vinegar, and mustard powder.

2. Turn the food processor on and, while the processor is running, gently stream in (and this is a really fine stream of oil . . . almost dripping) the oil. (I combine both of my oils into one measuring cup to make the streaming easier.)

3. As more of the oil is added to the mixture, you'll begin to see the mayonnaise come together. Once all of the oil is added, you have mayonnaise.

4. Give it a taste and add salt and pepper as you like.

5. Store in the refrigerator for up to 2 weeks.

Salted Caramel Sauce

This sweet and salty caramel sauce goes perfectly with ice cream, cookies, cakes, cheesecakes, and of course, eating straight from the jar. This caramel sauce only takes about 10 minutes to make and does not require a candy thermometer. It's all done by eyeballing it. And trust me, it's simple. Just make sure you let the sauce cool completely—it thickens up a bit as it cools.

Makes 1 cup

**¼ cup plus 2 tablespoons organic virgin coconut oil
   (or use refined coconut oil if you prefer not to have
   a coconut flavor)**
¾ cup granulated sugar
1 cup heavy cream
1 teaspoon sea salt

1. Melt the oil in a 5-quart saucepan over medium heat.

2. Once the oil has melted, pour in the sugar. Begin whisking frequently until the sugar is melted and golden brown. (You may notice the sugar kind of clumping up a bit. Don't worry, just keep whisking.)

3. Remove from the heat and carefully whisk in half of the cream. The mixture will bubble violently, but keep whisking. Once combined, whisk in the remaining cream and salt.

4. Pour the caramel into a heat-proof container and let come to room temperature.

5. Cover and chill in refrigerator.

Note: You may need to slightly reheat the caramel before using it after it's been in the refrigerator awhile.

Summer Peach Crumble

Summertime is peach time, and what could be better than a peach dessert? Yes, I realize that this recipe calls for frozen peaches, but you could easily switch out fresh, peeled peaches for this dessert when they are in season. This peach crisp is easy to put together. It's a perfect dessert for a casual picnic or potluck. I love how crispy and crunchy the topping gets in the oven. It's a nice contrast to the warm, soft peaches underneath.

Serves 6

CRUMBLE

Organic virgin coconut oil, enough to coat the baking pan

2 (12-ounce) bags frozen peaches, thawed

3 tablespoons almond flour

1 teaspoon cinnamon

½ teaspoon ginger powder

TOPPING

¾ cup organic virgin coconut oil, melted

½ cup honey

1½ cups rolled oats (not instant oats)

½ cup chopped pecans

½ cup almond flour

½ teaspoon cinnamon

½ teaspoon salt

1. Preheat the oven to 350°F. Use some coconut oil to grease an 8-by-8-inch baking pan.

Continued

2. In a medium bowl, toss the peaches with the almond flour, cinnamon, and ginger. Set aside.

3. In a small bowl, whisk the coconut oil and honey together. Set aside.

4. In a large bowl, add the oats, pecans, almond flour, cinnamon, and salt. Stir to thoroughly combine everything.

5. Pour the coconut and honey mixture over the oat mixture, and stir until everything is coated.

   Spoon the peaches into the greased baking pan and spread into an even layer. Then spread the oat mixture, evenly, on top of the peaches.

6. Bake for 30 to 40 minutes, or until the topping is slightly browned.

7. Let the crumble rest for 15 to 20 minutes before serving.

Potato Rolls

These good ol' fashioned potato rolls are the stuff bread dreams are made of. They're light, fluffy, and totally satisfying when you're looking for some good bread. The secret to these rolls is potato—mashed potatoes to be precise. You don't have to worry about having a go-to mashed potato recipe in order to make these rolls. It's simply a peeled, boiled potato that's mashed. These are really easy to make—just a little time-consuming, because you need to let them rise twice. But they're so worth the wait.

Makes 16 rolls

2 large eggs

¼ cup granulated sugar

2 teaspoons salt

¼ cup plus 2 tablespoons organic virgin coconut oil (or use refined oil if you prefer not to have the coconut flavor)

1 cup loosely packed unseasoned mashed potatoes (no skins)

1 envelope active dry yeast

¾ cup lukewarm milk

4½ cups all-purpose flour

1. Knead all of the ingredients together using the dough hook in a stand mixer.

2. Once the dough comes together, place it in a large, lightly greased bowl. Place the bowl in a warm spot, cover

Continued

with a non–terry cloth towel, and let the dough rise for 90 minutes. The dough should almost double in size.

3. Deflate the dough by punching it down, and divide it into 16 balls. Make sure that the balls are smooth. (I do this by pulling the edges under, which makes the top and sides smooth.)

4. Place the rolls into a lightly greased 9-by-13-inch baking pan with little to no space in between each roll. Cover loosely with plastic wrap and place back into that same warm spot for 90 minutes. The rolls will almost double in size again.

5. Remove the plastic wrap and preheat the oven to 350°F.

6. Bake for 20 to 25 minutes, or until the rolls are golden on top.

7. Remove from the oven and let cool.

Buttering Toast

If your morning routine is getting a bit stale with buttered toast, why not mix it up a little bit? You can butter your toast with coconut oil and get great energy from it, along with a bit of a tropical flavor to start your day.

All you need to do is dip your knife into the organic virgin coconut oil and spread it on your toast, just like you would spread butter.

Note: Using a well-seeded bread makes it taste even better.

Cocoa Butter

Don't want to slather your toast with plain ol' coconut oil? This cocoa butter will give you a bit of a chocolatey flavor to go along with the coconut.

This might just become your favorite toast topping.

Makes ½ cup

½ cup virgin coconut oil
1 tablespoon cocoa powder
1 tablespoon powdered sugar
½ teaspoon vanilla extract

1. Add all ingredients to the bowl of a food processor. Buzz it until everything is well blended.

2. Scoop the mixture into a lidded jar and store on the counter or in the refrigerator.

3. Smear liberally on toast.

Rocky Road Fudge

Sometimes you just need a piece of chocolate to get you through your day. This Rocky Road Fudge is rich and chocolatey, but the flavor gets a little variation from the walnuts and marshmallows. Putting this fudge together only takes a few minutes. The bulk of the time is waiting for it to chill and solidify in the refrigerator. But once it's chilled, you'll know it was definitely worth the wait.

Makes 18 pieces

1 cup organic virgin coconut oil (or use refined coconut oil if you prefer not to have the coconut flavor)
1 cup unsweetened cocoa powder
½ cup honey
1 tablespoon vanilla extract
Pinch of kosher salt
¾ cup mini marshmallows
¾ cup chopped walnuts

1. In a heatproof bowl (preferably glass) that will fit over the top of a saucepan, add the coconut oil, cocoa powder, and honey.

2. Add an inch of water to the saucepan and place the bowl on top. Heat over medium heat.

3. Stir the coconut oil mixture as it melts, and continue to keep it over the heat until everything has melted.

4. Stir in the vanilla extract and salt. Add the marshmallows and walnuts and stir until everything is well combined.

5. Pour the mixture into a parchment-paper–lined 9-by-4-inch loaf pan. Spread mixture out so that it is evenly distributed in the pan.

6. Place the pan into the refrigerator for at least 1 hour. It may take longer to fully chill and harden.

7. Remove from the refrigerator and simply lift the fudge out of the pan by using the edges of the parchment paper.

8. Slice into squares.

Coconut Crispy Rice Treats

Who didn't love these crispy rice treats when they were a kid? And who's to say you can't enjoy them again as an adult? I'm all for these classic childhood recipes. Using coconut oil in these treats makes them a little less heavy-tasting than when you use all butter, but some of the butter is still in there for that rich, satisfying flavor you're looking for. I added a cup of coconut flakes to these to bring out even more of the coconut flavor.

Makes 24 squares

2 tablespoons organic virgin coconut oil (plus more for coating the pan)
2 tablespoons unsalted butter
1 (10½-ounce) package mini marshmallows
1 cup unsweetened coconut flakes
8 cups crispy rice cereal

1. Use some coconut oil to grease a 13-by-9-inch pan.

2. In a 5- or 6-quart saucepan, melt the coconut oil and butter. Once melted, stir in the marshmallows. Continue to stir the marshmallows until they melt. Add in the coconut flakes and crispy rice cereal.

3. Remove from the heat and stir until everything is combined.

4. Pour the crispy rice mixture into the prepared pan and use a silicone spatula to smooth the mixture into an even layer. Press down on the mixture to compact it into the pan.

5. Let cool and then cut into squares.

Chicken Curry

This chicken curry isn't too spicy (unless you prefer a spicy curry powder), but it's full of rich flavors. The apple and apricot give it a sweetness not typically found in most curry dishes. It also helps to lighten it up a bit. The virgin coconut oil helps bring out the rich coconut flavor in the coconut milk, which combines really well with the curry. I love to serve this over quinoa or jasmine rice.

Serves 4

2 tablespoons organic virgin coconut oil

1 medium onion, diced

2 small apples, diced

1 clove garlic, minced

¼ cup chopped dried apricots

Kosher salt and freshly ground black pepper, to taste

1 pound chicken breasts, cut into 1-inch pieces

2 teaspoons curry powder

Cayenne pepper (optional)

1 (14-ounce) can full-fat coconut milk

1. Heat the oil in a large sauté pan over medium-high heat.

2. Once the oil is hot, add onion, apples, garlic, and apricots to the pan. Also add a large pinch of kosher salt and a few grinds of black pepper. Stir and cook until everything has softened and turned translucent, about 5 to 7 minutes.

3. Add the chicken to the pan and sprinkle the curry powder and cayenne (if using) evenly over the ingredients in the pan. Continue stirring and cook until all sides of the chicken are seared, about 8 minutes.

4. Pour in the coconut milk (make sure to scrape the thick stuff off the lid and into the pan too) and continue cooking until the chicken is no longer pink inside and the liquid has slightly thickened.

5. Serve with quinoa or jasmine rice.

Coconut Lemongrass Sorbet

If you love coconut and ice cream, this recipe is going to be your new best friend.

With four different forms of coconut in it, you know it's going to have a strong coconut flavor, and the hint of lemongrass highlights the flavor even more. If you like chocolate and coconut, I highly recommend adding a cup of dark chocolate chips when you pour the mixture into the ice cream machine. This will give you a chocolate crunch with every bite. I like to serve this sorbet all by itself, but it's especially delicious served on top of a bed of fresh berries.

Makes 1 quart

1 stalk lemongrass (for a more pronounced flavor, use 2 stalks)

1 cup unsweetened coconut flakes

2 cups full-fat coconut milk (you'll need 2 cans to get enough milk for this recipe)

1 cup granulated sugar

½ cup coconut water

2 tablespoons organic virgin coconut oil

1. Trim the grassy end and hard end off the lemongrass, which will leave you with the white part. Peel off the outermost layer. Chop the remaining lemongrass stalk into ½-inch rounds. (For a stronger lemongrass flavor, use 2 stalks of lemongrass.) Set aside.

Continued

2. Toss the coconut flakes into a sauté pan and toast them over medium heat. Stir them so that they don't burn. Take them off the heat once the flakes turn light brown in spots.

3. Add all of the ingredients to a medium saucepan. Bring the contents of the pan to a simmer, and stir until the sugar and coconut oil have melted.

4. Remove from the heat and let cool to room temperature.

5. Once cooled, strain the liquid into a large bowl. Cover the bowl and slide into the refrigerator to chill for 2 to 4 hours. It should be cold before it goes into the ice cream maker.

6. Pour the coconut mixture into the bowl of an ice cream maker and follow the manufacturer's instructions.

7. Remove from the ice cream machine and put into a freezer-safe bowl. Cover and freeze for at least 2 hours before serving.

Note: This sorbet won't get rock-hard in the freezer because of its fat content.

Frosting

A simple frosting recipe is so handy when you want to decorate cake or cookies, but finding that simple recipe can be difficult. This two-ingredient frosting recipe is just what you need when you're whipping up a cake or cookies at the last minute.

Makes 2 cups

½ cup organic virgin coconut oil (or use refined coconut oil if you prefer not to have the coconut flavor)
2 cups powdered sugar

Add the coconut oil and sugar to a large bowl and use a hand mixer (or a stand mixer) to blend everything together.

Note: If you're making this on a hot day, you may find that the frosting is quite runny, so I recommend using this recipe during the colder months of the year.

Cauliflower Fried "Rice"

Fried rice is a big hit at our house. It's something we regularly order from our favorite Chinese restaurant. Sometimes I want to eat a bit healthier but still crave the flavor of fried rice. That's where cauliflower "rice" comes in. Does it taste exactly the same? No, but with everything else going on in this dish, it doesn't really have to. You still get the overall feeling of eating fried rice without the heaviness that you can get from grain. I offer directions on how to make the cauliflower rice at the end of the recipe, but you can buy it already made at the store if you don't want to go through the work of making it.

Serves 4

3 large eggs

2 tablespoons organic virgin coconut oil (plus more for cooking the eggs)

3 chicken thighs, cut into 1-inch pieces

3 teaspoons sesame oil

Kosher salt and freshly ground black pepper, to taste

1 large yellow onion, diced

2 cloves garlic, minced

1 cup mixed frozen peas and carrots

4 cups cauliflower "rice" (see Note)

6 green onions, sliced thin

2 tablespoons soy sauce

1. Whisk the eggs together in a small bowl and set aside.

2. Lightly oil a large sauté pan with some coconut oil and heat over medium heat. Once the pan is hot, add the eggs and cook until the eggs are done and no longer jiggle when you shake the pan. Don't stir the eggs; just let them cook in a single layer.

3. Remove the eggs to a plate and let cool. Once cooled, slice the eggs into small strips.

4. In a medium bowl, toss the chicken with the sesame oil, salt, and pepper.

Continued

5. Heat 2 tablespoons of coconut oil in the same large sauté pan and heat over medium-high heat. 6. Once the oil is hot, sauté the chicken until lightly golden on all sides, about 5 minutes.

7. Add the onion and garlic to the pan and stir. Cook for 3 to 4 minutes, or until the onion has softened. Stir in the peas and carrots and cook for 1 to 2 minutes, just enough to thaw.

8. Add the cauliflower rice and green onions (reserve some of the green onion tops for garnish) to the pan and toss until it becomes hot.

9. Drizzle soy sauce over the mixture and stir to thoroughly combine.

10. Remove from the heat, stir in the egg strips, and top with the green onion garnish.

Note: To turn cauliflower into "rice," remove its core and cut into florets. Grate the florets on the large holes of a box grater over a large bowl or use the grating disc of your food processor.

Chocolate Bites or Bars

I bet you didn't know you could make your own chocolate bars. I call this recipe Chocolate Bites or Bars because you can either pour the chocolate into molds for bites, or you can pour the chocolate out onto a lined baking sheet, chill it and then break the chocolate into bars.

With only five ingredients and a few minutes, you can make yourself some good-for-you dark chocolate. This recipe fulfills any chocolate craving you may have.

Makes approximately 1 cup (depending on size of mold)

½ cup organic virgin coconut oil
½ cup unsweetened cocoa powder
¼ cup honey
½ teaspoon vanilla extract
Tiny pinch Kosher salt

1. In a heatproof bowl (preferably glass) that will fit over the top of a saucepan, add the coconut oil, cocoa powder, and honey.

2. Add an inch of water to the saucepan and place the bowl on top. Heat over medium heat.

3. Stir the coconut oil mixture as it melts and continue to keep it over the heat until everything has melted. Add the vanilla and salt and stir until the salt is thoroughly combined. Make sure that there are no clumps of cocoa.

Continued

4. For bites, pour the chocolate into silicon molds if making molded chocolate.

5. For bars, pour the chocolate onto a parchment-paper–lined baking sheet. Use an offset spatula to smooth the chocolate into an even layer.

6. Place the silicone molds or baking sheet into the refrigerator for at least 2 hours to firm up the chocolate.

7. Remove from the refrigerator and pop out of the molds or break into pieces.

8. Store in the airtight container in the refrigerator.

Cinnamon Rolls

What's better for breakfast on a cold morning than a hot cinnamon roll? These cinnamon rolls might look complicated, but they're really not. While there are quite a few ingredients and steps to make these rolls, nothing that you need to do for this recipe is hard. Topping the rolls off with a powdered sugar glaze takes them over the top, but I suppose you *could* also top them off with a scoop of vanilla ice cream for an even grander way of eating them.

Makes 16 rolls

CINNAMON ROLLS

1 cup whole milk

3 tablespoons organic virgin coconut oil (plus more for coating the dough-rising bowl and the pan)

3½ cups all-purpose flour

½ cup granulated sugar

1 large egg

2¼ teaspoons rapid-rise yeast (from 2 envelopes yeast)

1 teaspoon salt

FILLING

¾ packed cup light brown sugar

2 tablespoons cinnamon

¼ cup virgin coconut oil

ICING

½ cup powdered sugar

1 tablespoon whole milk

Continued

For the Rolls:

1. Add the milk and coconut oil in a glass measuring cup
   and put into the microwave, on high, until the coconut oil
   melts and the mixture is just warmed to 120°F to 130°F.
   Do this in 30-second increments, stirring the mixture
   between each session.

2. Pour the milk mixture into the bowl of a stand mixer
   fitted with a paddle attachment. Add 1 cup of the flour,
   sugar, egg, yeast, and salt to the bowl.

3. Beat on a low speed for 3 minutes and stop from time to
   time to scrape down the sides of the bowl.

4. Add the remaining 2½ cups of flour and continue to beat on low (you can increase the speed of your mixer to keep up with the consistency) until the flour is absorbed and the dough is sticky, scraping down the sides of the bowl.

5. If the dough is still really sticky, add a bit more flour (a tablespoon at a time) until the dough begins to form a ball and pulls away from the sides of the bowl. It will still be slightly sticky to the touch.

6. Turn the dough out onto a lightly floured work surface and knead until smooth and elastic, adding more flour if sticky, for about 4 minutes. Form the dough into a ball.

7. Lightly coat a large bowl with coconut oil. Drop the dough into the bowl and turn it over to coat the whole thing.

8. Cover the bowl with plastic wrap, then with a kitchen towel. Let the dough rise in a warm draft-free area until it has doubled in size, about 2 hours. Once the dough finished rising, continue the recipe.

For the Filling:

1. Preheat the oven to 375°F. Mix the brown sugar and cinnamon together in a bowl and set aside.

2. Lightly grease an 8-by-8-inch pan with coconut oil and set aside.

3. Punch down the dough in the bowl and slide the dough onto a lightly floured work surface. Roll out to a 24-by-18-inch rectangle.

Continued

4. Spread the ¼ cup of coconut oil over the dough, using an offset spatula. Sprinkle the cinnamon sugar evenly over the coconut oil.

5. Carefully cut 16 1-inch strips out of the dough. (Cut the strips the long way.)

6. Roll the strips to form each cinnamon roll, then place the roll into the greased pan. The rolls will be slightly crowded in the pan, but that's okay.

7. Bake for 15 to 20 minutes, or until the tops are golden brown.

8. Remove from heat and let cool before icing.

For the Icing:

1. Add the powdered sugar to a medium bowl. Add the milk and stir to combine.

2. Continue adding a little bit of milk at a time until you reach the desired consistency.

3. Drizzle or pour over the top of the cinnamon rolls.

Pear Maple Tart

This pear maple tart is perfect for fall. Its maple, pear, and cinnamon flavors are just right for those cooler days. Making this tart couldn't be easier. Everything but the pears goes into the mixer and then straight into the pan. Top with pear halves and you're ready for the oven.

I like making this for Thanksgiving. It's a different kind of dessert to put out among all the pies.

Serves 6 to 8

½ cup virgin coconut oil (plus more for tart pan)

1 cup all-purpose flour

½ teaspoon cinnamon

¼ teaspoon baking powder

½ cup granulated sugar

2 tablespoons light brown sugar, plus more for dusting

¼ cup grade B maple syrup, plus more for brushing on top

1 large egg

3 small pears (such as Seckel pears), peeled, halved, and cored

1. Preheat the oven to 350°F. Use the coconut oil to grease a 14-inch rectangular tart pan and set aside.

2. In a medium bowl, whisk the flour, cinnamon, and baking powder together. Set aside.

3. In a stand mixer, cream the coconut oil and sugars together. Add in the maple syrup and egg, and beat until everything is well combined.

4. Slowly add the flour mixture to the creamed mixture. Mix until they are thoroughly combined. You'll notice that the dough is really soft. It's supposed to be like that.

5. Add the dough to the prepared pan and use your fingers to push it around and evenly spread it into the pan and up the sides. You can flour your fingers to do this if you find the dough too sticky.

6. Lay the pear halves onto the dough, cut side down. Sprinkle the tops of the tart and the pears with brown sugar.

7. Bake for 45 minutes or until the crust is golden brown.

8. Once you remove the tart from the oven, brush it with some maple syrup. Serve warm or cooled.

Shrimp Fried Rice

What could be better for a weeknight dinner than a one-pan, 20 minute meal? In my book, not much. This Shrimp Fried Rice might just become your go-to weeknight recipe. I used shrimp, but to mix things up a bit, you could toss in pieces of chicken or tofu and follow the same directions. If you don't want to cook your own rice, you can use two pouches of ready-to-serve rice. To make things even easier, you don't even need to thaw the frozen peas and carrots. If you want even more variety in this dish, feel free to toss in some edamame or corn.

Serves 4

3 tablespoons organic virgin coconut oil

1 pound fresh medium shrimp (U21–23), peeled and deveined

1 medium yellow onion, diced

1 cup mixed frozen peas and carrots (could also add frozen corn and/or edamame)

2 cloves garlic, minced

½ teaspoon ginger powder

4 eggs, lightly beaten

4 cups cooked rice (I used jasmine rice)

3 green onions, sliced into thin rounds

2 tablespoons sesame oil

3 to 4 tablespoons soy sauce

1. Add the coconut oil to a large skillet and melt over medium heat. Once the oil has melted, add the shrimp.

2. Cook the shrimp for approximately 3 minutes per side or until they are cooked through. Remove the shrimp to a plate and set aside.

3. Add the onion to the skillet and cook until translucent, about 5 minutes. Add peas and carrots to the pan and cook until they begin to soften. Add in the garlic and ginger and stir. Cook for 1 minute.

4. Push the vegetables to one side of the pan and add the eggs to the other side of the pan. Scramble the eggs as you cook them.

5. Add the shrimp back into the pan along with the rice and most of the green onions. Drizzle with sesame oil and soy sauce. Stir to combine and cook until the shrimp are heated through.

6. Garnish with the remaining green onions.

Jalapeño Poppers Dip

This easy appetizer recipe takes all the delicious flavors of Jalapeño Poppers and turns them into a delicious scoop-able bite. Quick, easy, and oh-so addictive, this perfect party dip works all year round, but it is especially good during football season. There are no strange ingredients in this dish, and everything is easy to put together. In fact, it takes about 5 minutes. The longest part of making this Jalapeño Poppers Dip is waiting for it to cook. You can serve this dip hot or cold—it doesn't matter. Either way, it tastes delicious.

Makes 3 cups

2 (8-ounce) packages cream cheese, room temperature

1 cup mayonnaise (store-bought or homemade, see page 78)

1½ cups shredded cheddar cheese (I use medium sharp)

1 (4-ounce) can chopped jalapeños, drained

½ cup Panko bread crumbs

½ cup shredded Parmesan cheese

3 tablespoons organic virgin coconut oil

1 jalapeño, sliced

1. Preheat oven to 350°F. Blend the cream cheese and mayonnaise together in a mixing bowl (a stand mixer is easiest). Stir in the cheddar cheese and jalapeños.

2. Spoon into a 6-by-6-inch or 8-by-8-inch square baking pan. (If you use the 6-by-6-inch pan, you'll have a little left over.)

3. Combine the Panko bread crumbs and Parmesan cheese in a bowl.

4. Melt the coconut oil in a small container, then pour it into the bowl of Panko and cheese. Stir to thoroughly combine.

5. Evenly sprinkle the Panko mixture on top of the cheese mixture.

6. Pop into the oven and bake for 25 to 30 minutes, or until the topping is golden brown.

7. Top with slices of jalapeño.

Oven-Baked Sweet Potato Fries

Ahhhhh... sweet potato fries. I love the salty sweet flavor of these. This recipe will give you fries that have that soft and creamy inside with a hint of crisp on the outside. Remember, these aren't fried... they're oven-baked. If *sweet* sweet potato fries are your thing, I've given you that option in this recipe too. Because you use refined coconut oil in this recipe, there isn't a coconut flavor to these fries. You could use virgin coconut oil, but the benefits of using it are lost due to the high heat used to cook these fries.

Serves 4

2 large sweet potatoes
**3 tablespoons refined coconut oil (plus more to coat the
    baking sheet)**
Sea salt

1. Fill a 4- to 5-quart saucepan with water and place it on a burner.

2. Peel the potatoes and slice into ¼-inch square slices, dropping them into water. Bring the pot to a boil and reduce the heat to a slow rolling boil. Boil the potatoes for 2 minutes.

3. Preheat the oven to 450°F. Remove the potatoes from the water with a slotted spoon and put them on a cooling rack, so that the water can drip away.

4. Add the coconut oil to a large bowl and carefully drop the potatoes into the bowl.

5. Line a baking sheet with foil and then grease the foil with coconut oil. This step is really important. If you don't line the baking sheet, you'll be scraping the potatoes off of it.

6. Use your hands to thoroughly coat the potatoes with oil, then arrange the potatoes in a single layer on a baking sheet. Make sure there is also room between the potatoes.

7. Liberally toss the sea salt onto the potatoes.

8. Bake for 15 minutes, then gently turn the potatoes over and cook for another 15 minutes. Check the potatoes for doneness. They should have brown spots on them where their sugars have caramelized and formed crispy spots. If you don't see much of this, cook for another 5 to 6 minutes.

Note: For a sweet version, you could eliminate the salt and sprinkle the potatoes with a cinnamon-sugar mixture when they come out of the oven.

White Chocolate Coconut Bars

If you love coconut, these coconut bars are for you. The only thing standing between you and a mouthful of tropical, sweet coconut is a layer of white chocolate. These bars taste better than any coconut candy bar you could buy. If you're a fan of dark chocolate and coconut, you could easily swap out the white chocolate for dark chocolate. But give the white chocolate-coconut combination a try. They're really delicious together.

Makes 16 bars

2½ cups unsweetened shredded coconut
¾ cup virgin coconut oil, melted
⅓ cup grade B maple syrup
1 teaspoon vanilla extract
Pinch of Kosher salt
1 cup white chocolate chips

1. In a medium bowl, mix the coconut, coconut oil, maple syrup, vanilla, and salt together. Make sure that everything is thoroughly mixed.

2. Line an 8-by-8-inch baking pan with parchment paper and let the edges hang over the sides of the pan.

3. Spoon the coconut mixture into the baking pan in an even layer. Use a spatula to press the mixture firmly into the pan. Place in the freezer for 15 to 20 minutes.

4. While the coconut mixture is chilling, melt the white chocolate. Pour chips into a bowl and microwave on high in 30-second intervals. After each heating, give the chocolate a stir to mix everything up. Continue heating and stirring until the chocolate is melted. Set the chocolate aside to cool.

5. Remove the coconut mixture from the freezer and spread the chocolate evenly on top of the coconut. Place the pan into the refrigerator for 45 minutes.

6. Remove the pan from the refrigerator and pull on the parchment paper to remove the chilled coconut mixture from the pan.

7. Use a sharp knife to cut into bars. You may need to rinse the knife under warm water between the cuts so that the cuts are clean and the chocolate doesn't break.

Energy Bites

Got that mid-day slump, or are you just craving something a little sweet? These energy bites are just what you need. They are loaded with great ingredients that will not only give you energy (coconut oil, hemp hearts, and chia seeds) but will also fill you up (almond butter). They're also a nice little treat (chocolate chips and coconut flakes). You can keep them in the refrigerator when it's warm out, or in your desk drawer when it cools down. They can get a bit melty in warmer weather.

Makes 24 energy bites

8 Medjool dates, pitted
½ cup creamy almond butter
2 tablespoons organic virgin coconut oil
½ teaspoon cinnamon
¼ cup hemp hearts
¼ cup chia seeds
⅓ cup unsweetened coconut flakes
⅓ cup dark chocolate chips
1 cup rolled oats

1. Drop the dates, almond butter, coconut oil, and cinnamon into the bowl of a food processor. Run the processor until the dates are reduced to tiny bits.

2. Spoon the date mixture into a medium bowl and add the remaining ingredients. Stir to thoroughly combine the ingredients.

3. Spoon out a tablespoon of the mixture into your hands and form it into a ball. Set the ball on a baking sheet. Once all of the energy bites are rolled and on the baking sheet, let them rest for a couple of hours to set.

4. Store in an airtight container.

Tropical Banana Cream Pie

Banana cream pie is so rich, creamy and full of banana flavor, that the addition of coconut oil makes it just that much more tropical. This banana cream pie is really easy to make. You can make it in stages and then put the whole thing together. Once you prepare it, you have to chill it for several hours. This helps the filling and cream topping set. It also helps moisture seep into the crust, so it becomes easier to cut precise pieces of the pie. If you don't let it chill enough, you can still cut it into pieces, but everything will run together. No matter—it still tastes terrific.

Makes 1 (9-inch pie)

CRUST

2½ cups finely crushed graham crackers

⅓ cup granulated sugar

4 tablespoons organic virgin coconut oil, melted

3 tablespoons butter, melted

FILLING

½ cup granulated sugar

¼ cup cornstarch

2 cups half and half

4 large egg yolks

2 tablespoons virgin coconut oil, melted

1½ teaspoons vanilla extract

4 to 5 bananas (for filling and topping)

2 cups heavy whipping cream

¼ cup granulated sugar

½ teaspoon vanilla extract

ADDITIONAL TOPPINGS

Unsweetened coconut flakes

For the Crust:

1. Preheat the oven to 375°F. In a medium bowl, mix the graham crackers, sugar, coconut oil, and butter. Mix to thoroughly combine. The mixture should hold together when you squeeze some into the palm of your hand.

2. Press the mixture into a 9-inch pie pan. Bake for 10 minutes.

3. Set aside and let cool completely.

For the Filling:

1. In a medium saucepan, combine the sugar and cornstarch. Use a whisk to mix the two ingredients together thoroughly. Add the half and half and egg yolks to a saucepan and whisk until combined.

2. Bring to a low boil over medium heat while whisking until the sugar has melted. Continue whisking the entire time the pan is on the heat. Remove from the heat and whisk in the coconut oil and vanilla.

3. Cool the filling completely.

Continued

4. Whisk to loosen the custard and then pour half of it into the crust.

5. Top this layer of custard with a layer of sliced bananas. They should completely cover the custard.

6. Pour the remaining custard on top of the bananas and spread into an even layer. Top with another layer of

bananas. Again, completely cover the custard with the bananas.

7. Cover with plastic wrap and slide into the refrigerator. Let chill for at least 4 hours. I chill mine overnight.

For the Topping:

1. Chill your mixing bowl in the refrigerator or freezer. The more chilled your bowl is, the easier it is to whip the cream.

2. Pour the heavy whipping cream into a mixing bowl and add the sugar and vanilla.

3. Beat until the cream forms stiff peaks (meaning that when you remove the beater from the cream, it forms a peak that stays standing up).

4. Remove the plastic wrap from the pie and top with whipped cream.

5. Toss the coconut flakes into a sauté pan and toast them over medium heat. Stir them so that they don't burn. Take them off the heat once the flakes turn light brown in spots.

6. Sprinkle the toasted coconut in the center of the pie.

7. Circle the coconut with a ring of sliced bananas.

8. Chill for 2 hours before serving.

Biscuits

Do you dream about light and flaky biscuits dripping with butter? Yeah, me too. I can't stop with just one, either. This easy biscuit recipe will help to cure your biscuit cravings, I promise. Swapping out coconut oil for butter in this recipe gives the biscuits the lightest taste of coconut. It's not overwhelming, though, because I still use buttermilk in this recipe. The buttermilk helps to give the biscuits that nice little tang your taste buds are expecting.

Makes 15 (2-inch) biscuits

2 cups all-purpose flour
1 tablespoon baking powder
1 teaspoon salt
1 teaspoon granulated sugar
¼ cup plus 2 tablespoons organic virgin coconut oil
¾ cup buttermilk

1. Preheat the oven to 425°F. Add the flour, baking powder, salt, and sugar to a large bowl and whisk to thoroughly combine all the ingredients.

2. Add the coconut oil to the dry ingredients. Use a pastry cutter or a fork to blend the coconut oil into the flour. You'll be left with small crumbles when it's all mixed together.

3. Pour in the buttermilk and mix until you get a soft and sticky dough. Add another tablespoon of buttermilk if the dough seems dry.

4. Knead the dough a couple of times to make sure everything is mixed together.

5. Lightly flour a flat surface and turn the dough out onto the flour. Roll the dough to a ½-inch thickness. Cut circles with a 2-inch round cutter.

6. Place the biscuits on a parchment-paper–lined baking sheet.

7. Bake for 10 minutes or until the dough has risen and is slightly golden on top.

Banana Coconut Breakfast Smoothie

This breakfast smoothie is full of all kinds of good-for-you ingredients. Not only is it good for you, but it tastes like you're eating a chocolate-covered banana for breakfast. Or as my husband likes to say, it's like having a milkshake for breakfast. The cashews are rich in iron, in which many people are deficient, along with copper, zinc, and manganese. Bananas are rich in potassium and also contain manganese. The chia seeds contain a lot of omega-3s, along with some protein and fiber. Flax seeds are high in fiber and antioxidants. Cocoa nibs have lots of fiber and antioxidants along with magnesium and potassium. The addition of coconut oil in this smoothie gives you a boost of energy and a healthy dose of fat to keep you going through the morning.

Makes 1 (12-ounce) glass

1 cup cashew (or other nut) milk
1 frozen banana, broken into pieces
1 small handful raw cashews
1 tablespoon chia seeds
1 tablespoon flax seeds (brown or golden)
1 tablespoon cocoa nibs
1 tablespoon virgin coconut oil, barely melted

Add all ingredients to a blender. Blitz until everything is smooth (about a minute and a half). Pour into a glass and serve.

Garlic Herb Roasted Potatoes

I don't know about you, but I'm always looking for new side dishes. These Garlic Herb Roasted Potatoes might become your new favorite way to eat potatoes. They are packed with flavor and very easy to make.

Makes 2 servings

2 pounds mini golds potatoes, quartered (you could also use any small potatoes)

2 tablespoons organic virgin coconut oil, melted

1½ teaspoons garlic powder

1½ teaspoons Kosher salt

1 teaspoon dried thyme

½ teaspoon freshly ground black pepper

Chopped fresh parsley, for garnish

1. Preheat the oven to 400°F. Toss all the ingredients together in a large bowl and make sure everything is well coated.

2. Dump the potatoes onto a large-rimmed baking sheet (to keep any excess coconut oil from leaking off the edges).

3. Roast until the potatoes are tender and the edges are crispy, about 30 to 40 minutes.

4. Top with the fresh parsley.

Raspberry Scones

What could go better with a hot cup of coffee or tea than a light and fluffy scone? These raspberry scones are just the right amount of sweet and tart to have with that cuppa. Once you make this recipe you'll be hooked—they're so easy to make!

Makes 8 scones

SCONE

2 cups all-purpose flour

½ cup granulated sugar

2 teaspoons baking powder

½ teaspoon cinnamon

½ teaspoon salt

½ cup virgin coconut oil

½ cup heavy cream

1 large egg

1 teaspoon almond extract

1 heaping cup raspberries

GLAZE

1 cup powdered sugar

3 tablespoons heavy cream

For the Scones:

1. Preheat the oven to 400°F. Line a baking sheet with parchment paper.

2. Add the flour, sugar, baking powder, cinnamon, and salt to

Continued

a large bowl and whisk to thoroughly combine all of the dry ingredients.

3. Add the coconut oil to the dry ingredients and cut it in with a pastry cutter or a fork. Once it's all cut in, you'll have what looks like crumbles.

4. In a small bowl, whisk the cream, egg, and almond extract together.

5. Add the wet ingredients to the dry ingredients and mix together until everything is moistened and the dough comes together. Gently fold in the raspberries.

6. Using your hands, turn the dough into a ball. This shouldn't take a lot of work to do, and you don't have to knead the dough.

7. Place the dough ball onto the center of the lined baking pan. Push the dough out into an 8-inch circle and cut into 8 wedges.

8. Separate the wedges so that there is some space between each of them. The dough will spread a little when it bakes.

9. Bake for 20 to 25 minutes, or until lightly golden on top.

10. Remove from the oven and allow to cool completely.

For the Glaze:

1. Add the powdered sugar to a small bowl and stir in the cream. Add more cream to get the desired consistency of the glaze.

2. Drizzle over the cooled scones.

Spiced Ranch Crackers

Looking for an easy snack or something to put out at a party? These spiced ranch crackers are perfect for such occasions. They don't require many ingredients, bake quickly, and can be served hot or cold. Sounds like the perfect party food, doesn't it? Plus, I guarantee you'll run out of these crackers if you don't make a double batch.

Serves 6 to 8 as a snack

1 (1-ounce) package powdered ranch dressing mix
¼ teaspoon garlic powder
¼ teaspoon red chili flakes
¼ cup refined coconut oil, melted
1 (9-ounce) package oyster crackers

1. Preheat the oven to 275°F.

2. In a large bowl, mix the ranch dressing mix, garlic powder, red chili flakes, and coconut oil. Whisk until thoroughly combined.

3. Add crackers to the ranch mixture in a bowl and stir to combine and thoroughly coat the crackers with the ranch mixture.

4. Spread crackers out into a single layer on a large ungreased baking sheet and bake for 15 minutes.

5. Remove from the oven and put into a bowl. Serve warm or cold.

Peanut Butter

While store-bought peanut butter is pretty great, making your own tastes even better.

You might wonder why someone would bother making their own peanut butter instead of just buying it. Well, for starters, it tastes fresher. Think about how long that jar has been sitting on the shelf. You can buy peanuts in bulk and make up the peanut butter and be eating it the same day. Definitely fresher. Plus, you only need three ingredients to make your own peanut butter.

Makes approximately 2 cups

2 cups plain roasted peanuts
¼ to ½ teaspoon Kosher salt, to taste
¼ cup organic virgin coconut oil, melted

1. Pour the nuts and salt into a food processor fitted with the metal blade (you can start light on the salt and add more later). Process the nuts until they look like crumbs.

2. Check to see that your processor isn't warm. If it is, let it rest for 5 minutes. Making peanut butter in the food processor can be taxing for your machine. You need to check it from time to time and let it cool down before continuing the process.

3. While the nuts are processing, drizzle in the oil. You will notice that the nuts go through several stages while

they're being turned into peanut butter. They'll get sandy-looking and clumpy, and then they'll smooth out into a butter consistency.

4. Give it a taste and add more salt if you need it. Give the processor another buzz if you've added additional salt, so that it gets blended throughout the peanut butter.

5. Scoop the peanut butter into a lidded jar and store it in the refrigerator. It will harden up a bit when it's in the refrigerator, but you'll still be able to spread it.

No-Bake Chocolate Coconut Stacks

This recipe is so simple. It requires seven ingredients and only one bowl gets dirty. I don't know about you, but that's my kind of recipe. These No-Bake Chocolate Coconut Stacks are full of coconut goodness and have a bit of almond butter thrown in just for good measure. After all, coconut and almond are a perfect match for one another. You could easily sub in peanut butter for the almond butter if you're looking for a chocolate-peanut butter combination instead.

Makes 12 stacks

⅓ cup dark chocolate chips

4 tablespoons creamy almond butter (do not use the
  all-natural almond butter, which needs to be stirred)

3½ tablespoons cocoa powder

1 tablespoon organic virgin coconut oil

1 tablespoon honey

1 teaspoon vanilla extract

½ cup unsweetened shredded coconut

1. In a heatproof bowl (preferably glass) that will fit over the top of a saucepan, add the dark chocolate chips.

2. Add an inch of water to the saucepan and place the bowl on top. Heat over medium heat.

3. Stir the chocolate chips as they melt, and continue to keep them over the heat until they have all melted.

4. Add the almond butter, cocoa powder, coconut oil, honey, and vanilla to the bowl and stir until everything melts and is combined.

5. Turn off the heat and fold in the shredded coconut.

6. Use a tablespoon to measure out the coconut mixture, and place on a parchment paper–lined baking sheet.

7. Place the baking sheet in the refrigerator to chill your coconut stacks. After about an hour, they should be chilled and solid.

8. Enjoy!

Oatmeal Cookies

What's not to love about oatmeal cookies? Okay, maybe the raisins, but there aren't any raisins in this recipe. These cookies are soft and chewy, just like you want a cookie to be. The coconut oil in these makes them taste a lot lighter than your traditional butter-based oatmeal cookie. I like to make a batch of these and pass them out. People are really surprised by their lightness, and they don't have an overly coconuty flavor to them.

Makes 24 cookies

1¾ cups rolled oats
¾ cup all-purpose flour
¾ teaspoon cinnamon
½ teaspoon baking soda
½ teaspoon salt
½ cup organic virgin coconut oil
2 tablespoons unsalted butter
⅓ cup packed light brown sugar
¼ cup grade B maple syrup
1 large egg
1 teaspoon vanilla extract

1. Preheat the oven to 350°F. In a large bowl, whisk together all of the dry ingredients.

2. In a separate bowl (or stand mixer), beat the coconut oil, butter, sugar, and maple syrup together until they are lightened in color. Beat in the egg and vanilla until everything is well combined.

3. Gradually stir or add the dry ingredients to the wet ingredients and continue mixing until thoroughly combined.

4. Line a baking sheet with parchment paper or use a silicone baking sheet.

5. Spoon out 1 tablespoon of the dough and set it on the lined baking sheet. Continue this process, leaving 1 inch between cookies, until the sheet is full.

6. Wet your first two fingers and gently press down the tops of the cookies. You can leave them slightly mounded or flatten them a bit more (whichever you prefer). These cookies don't really spread much.

7. Slide into oven and bake for 10 to 12 minutes, or until the edges are slightly golden brown.

8. Remove from the oven to cool completely.

Dog Treats

Coconut oil isn't just for you. Why shouldn't your furry friends receive the benefits of coconut oil, too?

For all the same reasons coconut oil is good for you, it is also good for your dog. Another benefit of coconut oil for your dog is for their fur. Coconut oil is really good for your dog's hair. It will make it nice and soft. These yummy treats will have your dog doing all kinds of tricks to get another one.

Makes 42 (2-inch-round) dog treats

2½ cups whole-wheat flour
1 teaspoon baking powder
2 large eggs
1 cup creamy almond butter
2 tablespoons organic virgin coconut oil
2 tablespoons honey
¼ cup water, plus more as needed

1. Preheat the oven to 350°F.

2. Combine the flour, baking powder, and eggs in the bowl of your stand mixer and beat until combined.

3. Add the almond butter, coconut oil, honey, and water to the flour mixture and beat until you form a firm dough. If the mixture is still crumbly, add an additional tablespoon of water. Continue to add water, by the tablespoon, until a firm dough is achieved.

4. On a lightly floured surface, roll out dough to a ½-inch thickness and cut out shapes.

5. Bake for 20 minutes or until golden brown. Store in an air-tight container.

Part Four

BEAUTY

Coconut oil isn't a cure-all, but it does seem to come pretty close, especially when you take a look at all of the things it can do.

When you think about coconut oil, probably one of the last things you think about is smearing it all over your face and/or body. But you should. Coconut oil is used in many beauty products. It's naturally antibacterial and antifungal, is an excellent moisturizer for skin, can penetrate hair better than other oils, and, best of all, smells good.

You don't need to consume coconut oil to get all the beauty benefits from it. You can use it on your hair and skin in so many beneficial ways.

Dilute Essential Oils

If you use essential oils, you may have noticed that you develop a sensitivity to the oils and can no longer use them. This sensitivity usually comes with red patches on your skin.

But all may not be lost. You may still be able to use your favorite oils by diluting them with coconut oil.

Add a tablespoon of organic virgin coconut oil to a small bowl and then a couple of drops of essential oil to the bowl. Stir to thoroughly combine everything.

Now apply the coconut oil and essential oil blend to your skin. The coconut oil will act as a soothing barrier for your skin so that it doesn't come into direct contact with the essential oil.

Several of the following recipes use essential oils. A note about essential oils: When using essential oils on your skin, make sure that you use sunscreen if you plan on going outside within 24 hours of application. Essential oils can make your skin more susceptible to burning. This includes the use of tanning beds.

Grapefruit Lip Balm

This lip balm is a soft balm that melts easily into your lips, making them nice and soft. It smells like grapefruit, so it also has a refreshing aroma. Smelling grapefruit is known to be uplifting, soothing, clarifying, and stress-relieving. I'm not claiming that a swipe of this balm will whisk away all of the stress in your life, but it can help to relax you, and your lips will be kissably soft.

Makes 4 (20-milliliter) lip balm pots

2 tablespoons shea butter
2 tablespoons organic virgin coconut oil
1 tablespoon beeswax pastilles
½ teaspoon sweet almond oil
10 drops grapefruit essential oil (make sure that it is edible)

1. In a heatproof bowl (preferably glass) that will fit over top of a saucepan, add shea butter, coconut oil, and beeswax.

2. Add an inch of water to the saucepan and place the bowl on top. Heat over medium heat.

3. Stir the coconut oil mixture as it melts, and continue to keep it over the heat until everything has melted. Remove from the heat.

4. Add the almond oil and grapefruit essential oil to the mixture and stir to combine.

5. Carefully pour into the lip balm pots and let cool completely.

Tinted Lip Balm

Looking for soft lips, but want a little color too? This lip balm recipe gives you just that: softness with a hint of color. While it requires an entire tube of lipstick, the color is softened by the other ingredients. Plus, remember, it's divided into four pots. I keep a pot of this in my purse for a quick swipe of color.

Makes 4 (20-milliliter) lip balm pots

2 tablespoons shea butter

2 tablespoons organic virgin coconut oil

1 tablespoon beeswax pellets

1 tube lipstick (your favorite color)

½ teaspoon sweet almond oil

1. In a heatproof bowl (preferably glass) that will fit over the top of a saucepan, add the shea butter, coconut oil, beeswax, and the lipstick cut into pieces.

2. Add an inch of water to the saucepan and place the bowl on top. Heat over medium heat.

3. Stir the coconut oil mixture as it melts, and continue to keep it over the heat until everything has melted. Remove from the heat.

4. Add the almond oil to the mixture and stir to combine.

5. Carefully pour into the lip balm pots and let cool completely.

Moisturizing Face Cream

Combining the antioxidant properties of coconut oil with the moisturizing, inflammation-fighting and skin-smoothing properties of shea butter gives you a moisturizer like no other.

Add in the hydrating properties of almond oil and the antimicrobial properties of tea tree oil and you have a moisturizer that does multiple good things for your skin. You'll be amazed at how easy this face cream is to make, and the skin results from using this simple cream are fantastic.

Makes ¼ cup

2 tablespoons organic virgin coconut oil
2 tablespoons shea butter
1 tablespoon sweet almond oil
2 to 3 drops tea tree oil

1. In a heatproof bowl (preferably glass) that will fit over top of a saucepan, add the coconut oil and shea butter.

2. Add an inch of water to the saucepan and place the bowl on top. Heat over medium heat.

3. Stir the coconut oil mixture as it melts, and continue to keep it over the heat until everything has melted. Remove from the heat.

4. Add the almond oil and tee tree oil to the mixture and stir to combine.

5. Carefully pour into a lidded jar and let cool completely.

Face Mask for Oily Skin

This Oily Skin Face Mask nourishes and hydrates skin cells while also protecting skin from damage and aging. It gently exfoliates to deep-clean pores. Here is a simple face mask that only requires three ingredients, all of which you probably have on hand.

Makes 1 mask

2 tablespoons organic virgin coconut oil
1 tablespoon full-fat plain yogurt
2 teaspoons apple cider vinegar

1. In a small bowl, mix all the ingredients together.

2. Apply in an even layer to your face and let sit for 15 to 20 minutes.

3. Rinse with warm water and pat dry with a clean, dry towel.

Skin Hydration Mask

The combination of soothing coconut oil, detoxifying honey, and antioxidant almond oil enriches your skin cells and helps the skin hydrate.

Makes 1 mask

2 tablespoons organic virgin coconut oil

2 teaspoons honey

1 teaspoon sweet almond oil

1. In a small bowl, mix all ingredients together.

2. Apply in an even layer to your face and let sit for 15 to 20 minutes.

3. Rinse with warm water and pat dry with a clean, dry towel.

De-Puffing Face Mask

This mask de-puffs and re-energizes tired and dull-looking skin by increasing blood flow and circulation. It exfoliates and sloughs off dead skin cells while enabling the soothing properties of coconut oil to hydrate your skin.

Makes 1 mask

2 tablespoons organic virgin coconut oil

1 tablespoon instant espresso powder

1. In a small bowl, mix all ingredients together.

2. Apply in an even layer to your face and let sit for 15 to 20 minutes.

3. Rinse with warm water and pat dry with a clean, dry towel.

Makeup Remover Pads

I'm always looking for a good makeup-remover pad, something that removes my makeup but doesn't strip my skin of its natural oils. These makeup remover pads remove the makeup, but leave your skin feeling soft and moisturized. Fractionated coconut oil is used here because it stays liquid in all temperatures, unlike virgin coconut oil. The tea tree oil has antimicrobial properties that help with acne.

2 tablespoons fractionated coconut oil
2 teaspoons baby wash
½ teaspoon tea tree oil
Boiled water cooled to room temperature

1. Fill a glass jar with cotton pads.

2. Mix the coconut oil with baby wash and tea tree oil.

3. Pour over the cotton pads. Pour enough water over the pads to just cover them.

4. Place the lid over the jar and shake to evenly distribute the liquid over all the pads.

Note: This is not meant to be an eye makeup remover. Keep the tea tree oil away from your eyes.

Honey Coconut Hair Mask

Looking for that glossy hair you see in magazines and on TV? This Honey Coconut Hair Mask might just be the thing that gives you that shiny hair. Coconut oil is structured such that it penetrates hair better than other substances can. It also helps hair maintain its protein. Because of this fact, this hair mask may not be for you. If you've got coarse, thick hair, your hair might be low in protein, and if that's the case, this mask may make your hair worse. Your hair would benefit from some other oil. If you've got thin to medium shiny hair, then this mask will probably give your hair more shine and volume.

Makes 1 mask

1 to 3 tablespoons organic virgin coconut oil (amount depends on length of hair)
2 tablespoons honey

1. Spoon the coconut oil and honey into a small saucepan and heat over low heat just until the coconut oil melts. Stir to combine everything.

2. Allow the mixture to cool until it's cool to the touch (not so long that the coconut oil hardens again).

3. Apply the mixture to either dry or wet hair. Focus on the ends and stay away from the scalp.

4. Let sit on the hair for 15 to 30 minutes. If your hair is long, make sure to tie it up, as the coconut oil will leave oil stains on clothes and furniture.

5. Shampoo and condition your hair as normal. You may notice that your hair feels a bit oilier than usual. This is normal when using coconut oil. If you use a shampoo with less surfactant, you'll notice this more.

Note: Be careful in the shower or tub after rinsing this, as the coconut oil may make the floor slippery.

Whipped Body Butter

Mango, coconut, and almond oil combine to make a super-moisturizing body butter. Whipping the mixture makes it feel light and fluffy and keeps it from feeling oily. You can mix various combinations of essential oils for this body butter, but I love the smell of eucalyptus with the lavender. Eucalyptus and citrus oils would be a pleasant combination too.*

Makes 1 cup

½ cup mango butter
¼ cup organic virgin coconut oil
¼ cup sweet almond oil
10 drops eucalyptus essential oil
10 drops lavender essential oil

1. In a heatproof bowl (preferably glass) that will fit over the top of a saucepan, add mango butter and coconut oil.

2. Add an inch of water to the saucepan and place the bowl on top. Heat over medium heat.

3. Stir the coconut oil mixture as it melts, and continue to keep it over the heat until everything has melted.

4. Remove from the heat and let cool for 15 minutes.

5. Stir in the almond oil and essential oils.

6. Place the bowl into refrigerator to chill. The oils should be partially solidified. (I chill mine for 1 hour.)

7. Using a stand or hand mixer, whip the coconut oil mixture until you get a glossy whipped-cream consistency.

8. Spoon body butter into a lidded jar.

Note: If you find while you're whipping that the mixture is not looking like whipped cream, you may need to pop it back into the refrigerator to chill a bit longer. Once it's chilled, go ahead and begin whipping it again.

*Citrus essential oils can make your skin more sensitive to sunlight, which can cause sunburn.

Foot Scrub

I love using this as a foot scrub, but you could use it as an all-over body scrub too. It's full of good-for-your-skin oils such as coconut, vitamin E, and tea tree oil. When Epsom salts are absorbed through the skin, they work to relieve muscle tension, pain, and inflammation in joints, which is perfect for aching feet.

Makes 2 cups

¼ cup organic virgin coconut oil
¼ cup vitamin E oil
10 to 12 drops tea tree oil
1 cup Epsom salts

1. In a heatproof bowl (preferably glass) that will fit over the top of a saucepan, add the coconut oil.

2. Add an inch of water to the saucepan and place the bowl on top. Heat over medium heat.

3. Stir the coconut oil as it melts and continue to keep it over the heat until everything has melted.

4. Remove from the heat and stir in the vitamin E and tea tree oils.

5. Put the Epsom salts into a medium bowl, pour the coconut mixture over the salts, and stir to mix.

6. Store in a lidded jar.

Note: Be careful when using this foot scrub, as it may make your shower or tub floor slippery.

Mustache and Beard Enhancer

Coconut oil can make your mustache or beard softer and help eliminate any dry skin you may experience underneath the beard hair.

Just like the hair on your head, coconut oil can make your mustache or beard hair shinier.

You can use coconut oil as a preshave oil to soften facial skin and hair. Simply apply a light layer of oil to your skin, then apply any shave cream you may be using.

Coconut oil is also an excellent postshave treatment. Because of its antimicrobial properties, coconut oil can help to prevent razor burn and ingrown hairs.

AROMATHERAPY

Combine a tablespoon of organic virgin coconut oil with your choice of essential oils, then dab onto your temples.

CHAMOMILE: mood lifter
LAVENDER: relaxation
LEMON: increases concentration and mental awareness
PEPPERMINT: stimulation
SANDALWOOD: relieves tension
YLANG-YLANG: relieves headaches

Fizzy Bath Bombs

Taking a hot bath is one of life's little luxuries. Add a pleasant-smelling Fizzy Bath Bomb to the tub and you've got yourself a superior experience. These Fizzy Bath Bombs not only smell great but are great for your skin too. The Epsom salts relax you by relieving muscle tension and pain; the coconut oil smoothes your skin; and the lemongrass essential oil is an antidepressant, antimicrobial, and fungicide, among many other benefits.

Makes about 3 cups

1 cup baking soda
½ cup citric acid
½ cup cornstarch
½ cup Epsom salts
1 tablespoon organic virgin coconut oil, melted
2 teaspoons water
15 to 20 drops lemongrass essential oil
2 drops food coloring (can use gel colorings in this recipe)

1. Mix all of the dry ingredients together in a large bowl.

2. Mix all of the wet ingredients together in a small bowl.

3. Slowly add the wet ingredients to the dry ingredients and whisk to thoroughly combine everything.

4. Spoon the mixture into silicone molds and pack down firmly with the back of a spoon. Be careful not to overpack the mold: as the bombs dry, they may expand in the molds.

5. Let dry in the molds for 24 to 48 hours before carefully removing from the molds.

Note: If you are using the traditional ball-shaped molds for making these bath bombs, you may need to play with the moisture a bit. The mixture should be just barely wet but still hold together when you pinch some together between your fingers.

To Brighten the Appearance of Skin

Have you noticed that your skin is looking a bit dull? Coconut oil can help with that too.

Mixing coconut oil with baking soda for an all-natural exfoliant can help brighten the look of your skin.

Makes 1 application

1 tablespoon organic virgin coconut oil
½ tablespoon baking soda

1. Mix the coconut oil and baking soda together until they are thoroughly combined.

2. Apply to your face and gently rub in circular motions.

3. Rinse with warm water and blot your face dry with a clean, dry towel.

Help Get Rid of Dandruff

Dandruff is linked to an increase of lipophilic yeasts of the genus Malassezia. This can cause your scalp to be itchy and flaky. A natural way that you can help rid yourself of dandruff is with coconut oil. Since coconut oil is an antifungal, antimicrobial oil, rubbing it into your affected scalp should help alleviate the dandruff.

Makes 1 application

2 tablespoons organic virgin coconut oil

1. Melt a couple of tablespoons of virgin coconut oil. Make sure that you've let the oil cool to the point where it's comfortable for your skin.

2. Apply it to a clean scalp (wash and dry your hair first), especially around the crown area, and let it sit for 5 to 10 minutes. Rinse with warm water and let your hair air dry. You can also apply the coconut oil and leave it in overnight (cover your head so that you don't leave oil marks on your pillow), and then wash it out and dry your hair as usual.

Note: You will need to do this once a week until you no longer see flakes.

Massage Oil

Using coconut oil as a massage oil shouldn't come as a surprise, since it has so many health benefits. Its antimicrobial properties help skin rid itself of harmful bacteria and fungus that can grow on it. Coconut oil contains vitamin E, which is very beneficial to skin. It nourishes and makes skin smoother and softer. Its antioxidant properties help prevent aging of the skin.

All of these reasons make coconut oil a great massage oil. It also easily absorbs into the skin, so you get all of the benefits of the oil. Because of coconut oil's quick absorption factor, I've added almond oil to help maintain lubrication while massaging.

Makes 1 cup

1 cup fractionated coconut oil
2 tablespoons sweet almond oil
30 drops essential oil of your choice

1. Add all the ingredients to a small bowl and stir to combine.

2. Use a funnel to pour the mixture into a pump bottle.

Silky Smooth Shaving Cream

You can have smooth, soft legs even after shaving. Really! And it doesn't require ingredients you can't pronounce or that are bad for your health. With only a few simple ingredients, your legs can feel amazing and not suffer from razor burn.

Makes approximately ½ cup

4 tablespoons shea butter
3 tablespoons organic virgin coconut oil
2 tablespoons sweet almond oil
10 to 12 drops eucalyptus essential oil
2 teaspoons tea tree oil

1. Add the shea butter and coconut oil to a heatproof bowl (preferably glass) that will fit over the top of a saucepan.

2. Add an inch of water to the saucepan and place the bowl on top. Heat over medium heat.

3. Stir the coconut oil mixture as it melts and continue to keep it over the heat until everything has melted.

4. Remove from the heat and stir in the almond oil, essential oil, and tea tree oil.

5. Place the bowl into the refrigerator to chill. The oils should be partially solidified. (I chill mine for 1 hour.)

Continued

6. Using a stand or hand mixer, whip the coconut oil mixture until you get a glossy whipped cream consistency.

7. Spoon the shaving cream into a lidded jar.

Note: If you find while you're whipping that the mixture is not looking like whipped cream, you may need to pop it back into the refrigerator to chill a bit longer. Once it's chilled, go ahead and begin whipping it again.

Overnight Foot Moisturizer

Have your feet looking and feeling their best in no time. The coconut oil and the mango butter are super-moisturizing. The almond oil is rich with vitamin A, which encourages healthy skin cell production. The essential oils are good for your feet too. All you need to do is rub this on your feet at night and put on a pair of socks. Keep using it to keep your feet soft and smooth.

Makes approximately ½ cup

3 tablespoons organic virgin coconut oil
2 tablespoons mango butter
1 tablespoon beeswax pastilles
1 tablespoon sweet almond oil
5 drops peppermint essential oil
5 drops lavender essential oil

1. In a heatproof bowl (preferably glass) that will fit over the top of a saucepan, add the coconut oil, mango butter, and beeswax pastilles.

2. Add an inch of water to the saucepan and place the bowl on top. Heat over medium heat.

3. Stir the coconut oil mixture as it melts, and continue to keep it over the heat until everything has melted.

4. Once everything has melted, remove from the heat and let rest for 3 to 5 minutes. Stir in the almond and essential oils.

5. Pour moisturizer into a jar and let cool completely.

Foot Moisturizer for Cracked Heels

Are your feet so dry that your heels have cracked? This happens in both summer and winter, and it can be a real hassle. In the summer, your feet don't look so pretty in sandals, and in the winter, your heels can hurt because the cracked skin gets caught on your socks. This moisturizer should help remedy the problem. It's a bit stronger than the overnight foot moisturizer because it's made not only with coconut oil but shea butter as well. Shea butter is rich in oleic acid, which is not only a moisturizer but works to strengthen cell membranes and help repair damaged cells. Tea tree oil is an antimicrobial, anti-bacterial, and antifungal element that can help keep cracked heels from becoming infected.

Makes approximately 1¼ cups

¾ cup organic virgin coconut oil
½ cup shea butter
½ cup beeswax pastilles
2 tablespoons tea tree oil

1. In a heatproof bowl (preferably glass) that will fit over the top of a saucepan, add the coconut oil, shea butter, and beeswax pastilles.

2. Add an inch of water to the saucepan and place the bowl on top. Heat over medium heat.

3. Stir the coconut oil mixture as it melts, and continue to keep it over the heat until everything has melted.

4. Once everything has melted, remove it from the heat and let rest for 3 to 5 minutes. Stir in the tea tree oil.

5. Pour the moisturizer into a jar and let cool completely.

Luxurious Body Wash

Some recipes for coconut oil body wash call for virgin coconut oil. I prefer to use the fractionated because it stays liquid no matter the temperature. The honey is really good for your skin because it's antibacterial, chock-full of antioxidants, extremely moisturizing, and soothing to the skin. Castile soap is used to make this body wash because it's made from vegetable sources. It helps to moisturize your skin (and, combined with the coconut and almond oils, it makes for a super-moisturizing clean). You might find that this body wash is so moisturizing that you may not need to use lotion after your shower. I love using this Luxurious Body Wash so much, I've ditched my other soaps. This wash is also less expensive to make than buying other liquid soaps.

Makes 1¼ cups

¼ cup fractionated coconut oil

¼ cup honey

1 tablespoon sweet almond oil

1 teaspoon tea tree oil

20 drops eucalyptus essential oil

15 drops grapefruit essential oil

⅔ cup liquid Castile soap (unscented)

1. Add all of the ingredients to a medium bowl, except for the Castile soap, and whisk to combine.

2. Slowly add the Castile soap and gently whisk it into the rest of the ingredients. Don't be too rough with the whisking or you'll end up with a big bowl of bubbles.

3. Use a funnel to pour the mixture into your bottle.

4. Shake before using.

Relaxing Magnesium Body Butter

Magnesium works as a natural muscle relaxant, which is why many people use magnesium oil to help them sleep. This magnesium body butter also contains lavender, which is also used as a relaxant to help people sleep better. The coconut and shea oils in this body butter will help your skin accept the magnesium more easily (sometimes a straight application of magnesium oil can cause itchiness) and will also work to moisturize your skin.

Makes 1½ cups

½ cup organic virgin coconut oil

½ cup shea butter

¼ cup magnesium oil

¼ cup sweet almond oil

10 to 15 drops lavender essential oil

1. In a heatproof bowl (preferably glass) that will fit over the top of a saucepan, add coconut oil and shea butter.

2. Add an inch of water to the saucepan and place the bowl on top. Heat over medium heat.

3. Stir the coconut oil mixture as it melts, and continue to keep it over the heat until everything has melted.

4. Remove from the heat and let cool for 15 minutes.

5. Stir in the magnesium oil, almond oil, and essential oil.

6. Place the bowl into refrigerator to chill. Oils should be partially solidified. (I chill mine for 2 hours.)

7. Using a stand or hand mixer, whip the coconut oil mixture until you get a glossy whipped cream consistency.

8. Spoon magnesium body butter into a lidded jar.

Note: If you find while you're whipping that the mixture is not reaching a thick, creamy consistency, you may need to pop it back into the refrigerator to chill a bit longer. Once it's chilled, go ahead and begin whipping it again.

Part Five

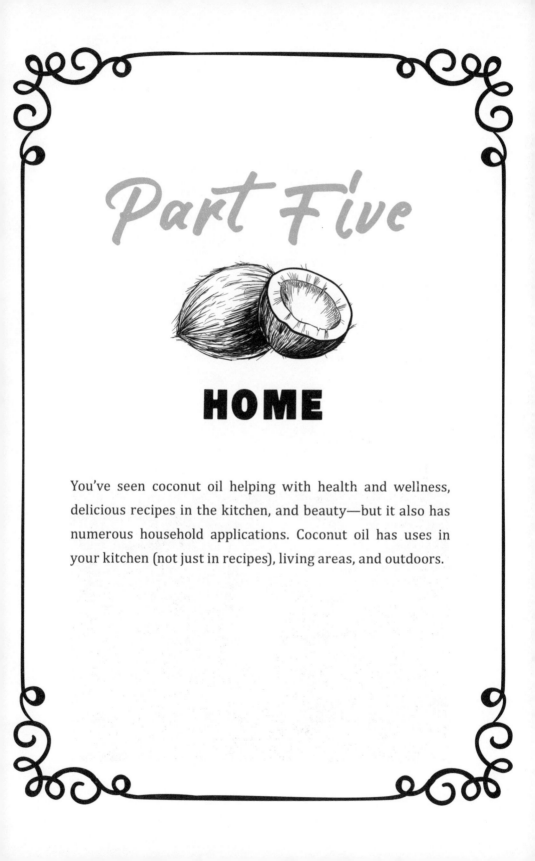

HOME

You've seen coconut oil helping with health and wellness, delicious recipes in the kitchen, and beauty—but it also has numerous household applications. Coconut oil has uses in your kitchen (not just in recipes), living areas, and outdoors.

Season a Cast-Iron Skillet

Cast iron is considered, by some, to be the holy grail of cooking instruments. The beautiful thing about cast-iron cookware is its durability. A cast-iron skillet, well cared for, will last for generations. I still have one of my grandmother's cast-iron skillets. But cast iron needs to be seasoned and cared for. One of the best oils for doing this is coconut oil. Seasoning cast iron is easy to do.

Makes 1 treatment

Refined coconut oil

1. Preheat the oven to 400°F. Use a paper towel to spread a thin coating of refined coconut oil all over the inside of the skillet (both the sides and the bottom).

2. Place the oiled pan on one of the upper racks of the oven and bake for one hour. Turn off the heat and let the pan cool in the oven.

3. Any time you cook in the pan, you need to clean it with a stiff plastic brush and hot water (no soap). Dry the pan and put it on a burner to get rid of any excess moisture. Turn off the heat and add a teaspoon of refined coconut oil to the pan. Use a paper towel to coat the sides and bottom of the pan and it will be ready to use the next time you pull it out.

Furniture Polish

Wood furniture can get dull and dusty-looking when it gets older. A sure way to brighten it up is with a buff of coconut oil. Has the grain or color dulled? Using coconut oil can help to bring new life to your furniture.

Makes ½ cup

½ cup organic virgin coconut oil
2 tablespoons fresh lemon juice

1. Combine coconut oil and lemon juice together in a wide-mouth container.

2. Before using polish, test the polish on an inconspicuous spot.

Continued

3. Use a soft polishing cloth and dip into the polish. Polish wood furniture by rubbing briskly with the grain of the wood.

4. Let the wood rest for 30 to 45 minutes so that the coconut oil can be absorbed into the wood, after which point you can put your things back on the wooden surface.

Crayon Buster

When your kids make your walls their personal canvas, don't sweat it.

Apply a little coconut oil (refined or virgin) to a cotton ball and wipe down the drawings. The oil breaks down the wax on the crayons. Do not, however, use this trick on wallpaper, as it will leave a grease mark.

Note: Coconut oil also removes ink from walls, plastic, and vinyl. (Use that same cotton ball trick to remove it.)

Stuck Zipper

Got a stuck zipper? Stop pulling on it and lubricate it. Rub a small dab of coconut oil on the zipper teeth to help it glide smoothly along.

Remove Sticky Labels

Do you have a bottle that has a label stuck to it that you just can't remove? Short of using a chisel, labels can be next to impossible to get off. That's where coconut oil comes into play.

Makes any desired amount

Refined or organic virgin coconut oil
Baking soda

1. Remove as much of the label as you can and then wash the bottle/container and label with hot soapy water, again removing as much of the label as you can.

2. Wipe the bottle/container dry.

3. Dab a little bit of coconut oil (refined or virgin will work) on what remains of the label and sprinkle some baking soda over the coconut oil.

4. Rub the bottle/container with a dry paper towel and all of the label bits that were left should be gone.

5. When all the bits are gone, wash the bottle/container with warm soapy water.

Wooden Cutting Board Conditioner

Wooden cutting boards should be cleaned with hot soapy water and not soaked, as this will cause them to crack and warp. If you've been cutting meat on your wooden cutting board, you will want to also wash it off with a weak bleach solution or hydrogen peroxide.

To maintain your wooden cutting board, you should periodically condition it with oil. Depending on how much you use your board, this could be monthly or as little as twice a year. The oiling of the board helps to maintain the board's surface and helps to keep it from cracking.

The oil you use should be food-grade fractionated coconut oil, because it's not prone to going rancid. Double check when you buy your oil that it is food-grade—not all fractionated coconut oil is.

Before you oil your board, make sure that it is clean. Give it a good washing in hot soapy water. The board also needs to be completely dry before oiling. Oil the board using a clean, soft cloth, and wipe the board evenly with the oil, letting it soak in. I like to let the oil soak in overnight, then wipe any excess oil off in the morning.

Note: This also works on wooden utensils.

Kitchen Helper

Before measuring sticky stuff, such as peanut butter or corn syrup, wipe down your measuring cup or spoon with a little bit of coconut oil (refined or virgin). Your ingredients will slide right off, and you'll get a correct measurement of the ingredient.

Rust Remover

Yep, you can use coconut oil to help remove rust from your favorite knives, scissors, or utensils. All you need to do is rub a nice coating of coconut oil on the rusty metal and let sit for an hour. After an hour, use a clean, dry cloth to rub the coconut oil and rust away.

Got Scuffs?

Do you have those annoying black scuff marks on your floor? Coconut oil to the rescue, again. Those scuff marks can be buffed away with a combination of equal parts coconut oil (refined or virgin) and baking soda. Just apply to a soft cloth and buff the marks away.

Camp Fire Starter

Instead of using lighter fluid to get the camp fire started, use coconut oil. Simply soak some cotton balls in melted organic virgin coconut oil and store them in a zip top bag. When you're ready to get the fire going, pull apart the cotton balls and tuck them into the kindling wood. Give the cotton balls a light. They should burn for about 5 to 10 minutes each, which should get your fire started beautifully.

Dish Washing

You might be wondering how in the world coconut oil can help with dish washing, but it can. Got some really stuck-on food on your plates or baking pans? Rub some coconut oil on the stuck food and wait a few minutes. Without much effort at all, you'll be able to wash away that stubborn food that, a few minutes ago, seemed like it needed a hammer and chisel to get off.

Squeaky Hinges

Instead of using something such as WD-40 on your squeaky hinges, try coconut oil. Just a little bit of refined or organic virgin coconut oil wiped on the hinge will help get rid of those squeaks.

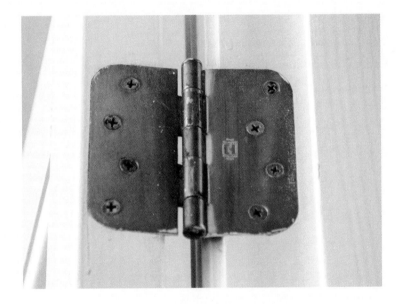

Metal Faucet Polish

Faucets looking a little less than fresh?

Take a dab of coconut oil and a clean, dry cloth and rub the faucet with the coconut oil. You'll have the finish on the faucet looking brand new. It will even help to clean the crud out of the crevices.

Cosmetic Brush Cleaner

Using coconut oil to clean your makeup brushes leaves them nice and clean and conditions them so they stay soft and supple. The tea tree oil adds an antimicrobial element.

Makes any desired amount

Water
2 parts liquid antibacterial soap
1 part fractionated coconut oil
¼ teaspoon tea tree oil

1. Add water to a wide-mouthed jar that will hold all of your brushes—just enough to cover the brush part. You may need to use a bowl if you've got a lot of brushes.

2. Pour in the soap, coconut oil, and tea tree oil, then give everything a good stir to mix it all up.

3. Dip the bristle end of your brushes into the mixture and give them a good swish. Soak for 2 to 3 hours.

4. Remove the brushes, then dump out the mixture. Rinse the jar, or bowl, in water, then refill it with clean water. Dip your brushes back into the water and swish them around. Gently massage the brushes with your hands to help remove any makeup that may still be hiding in them.

5. Remove the brushes and rinse them with cool water.

6. Dry in a single layer on a paper towel overnight.

Soap Scum Remover

You can use harsh chemicals to get rid of soap scum or you can use coconut oil to get rid of that film on your shower or bathtub.

Refined or organic virgin coconut oil
White vinegar

1. Clean that soap scum off your shower/bathtub by putting a dab of refined or organic virgin coconut oil onto a damp cloth and wipe the area down.

2. Once you're done wiping with the coconut oil, spray the area with white vinegar and wipe that down with a clean cloth.

3. Make sure that you wipe all the coconut oil off with the vinegar so that your shower or tub isn't slippery.

Gardening

Just as you can use coconut oil to keep ingredients from sticking to your measuring cups and spoons, you can also use coconut oil to keep your gardening tools free from clinging dirt.

Simply coat your tools with a light coating of refined or organic virgin coconut oil, and your tools will stay relatively clean while you're digging in the dirt.

Water Mark Preventer

Got a beautiful stainless steel sink that looks terrible after using it a couple of times? Coconut oil can help fix that.

Rub a small amount of coconut oil all around the sink to help prevent those ugly water marks. Your sink will have a clean sparkle to it.

For Your Car

You've washed your car, but despite this, do you find you still have bugs stuck to it? Or maybe you've parked under a tree and got nasty tree sap stuck to your car? If elbow grease isn't enough to get it off, coconut oil can do the job.

Just apply a dab of coconut oil to those bugs and/or sap and let it sit for a few minutes, then take a clean, dry cloth and rub it right off.

INDEX